Rev. A. Ettenhofer

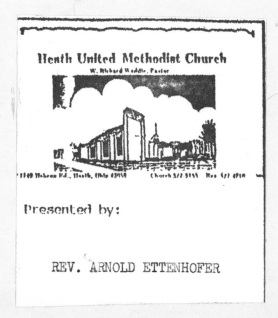

Heath United Methodist Church

W. Richard Waddle, Pastor

7149 Hebron Rd., Heath, Ohio 43056   Church 522-5151   Res. 522-4918

Presented by:

REV. ARNOLD ETTENHOFER

MAN IN THE MIDDLE

MAN IN THE MIDDLE

CONVERSATIONS OF

A TEMPTED SOUL WITH TWO

VOICES ON

THE SEVEN DEADLY SINS

BY

JAMES A. PIKE

AND

HOWARD A. JOHNSON

THE

Seabury Press *GREENWICH · CONNECTICUT*

1956

© 1956 by The Seabury Press, Incorporated

Library of Congress Catalog Card Number: **56-7970**

Design by P. Atkinson Dymock

Printed in the United States of America

TO OUR PARENTS

PREFACE

Only recently has the word *sin* found its way back into the vocabulary of sophisticated conversation. During the long eclipse of the word, the reality persisted nevertheless, and as to the forms it takes, there appears to have been no substantial change over the years. For this reason the centuries-old classification of the Seven Deadly Sins, although never entirely satisfactory, is still useful today.

It was on this assumption that the three-cornered conversations, which form the bulk of this volume, were prepared for presentation as trialogues at Sunday Evensong in the Cathedral of St. John the Divine during July, 1954, and for broadcast *seriatim* over the ABC Radio Network on Sunday evenings in July and August. Participating in the trialogues, in addition to the authors, was Ralph E. Hartwig, Lay Reader of St. Peter's Church, Peekskill, New York, and member of the Council of the Diocese of New York, who took the role of the tempted soul. To him we are greatly indebted not only for his generous gift of talent and time but also for his many constructive suggestions as to the script. We are also grateful for the ready co-operation of Wiley Hance, manager of public affairs for the American Broadcasting Company, and William J. Moll, director of public relations for the Cathedral.

These conversations are intended as a dramatic externalization of the inner debates of the soul. This method of exposition has obvious limitations but in a measure corresponds to reality, inasmuch as the soul under temptation does seem to be caught in the cross fire of conflicting counsel. Therefore, in preparing the manuscript for publication, we have largely preserved the casual style and colloquialism of the original scripts and have retained the brevity—and, hence, the incompleteness—necessitated by the time limits of the two media of their oral presentation. It need hardly be said that these chapters are not offered as a textbook on Christian ethics or as a systematic exposition of moral theology. Nonetheless, their reception by the cathedral congregation and radio audience gives us reason to hope that the trialogues may assist some readers to know themselves better and perhaps lead them to some deeper reflection on their duty to God and neighbor—and even to a recognition of man's need of something more than ethics.

J. A. P.

H. A. J.

The Cathedral Close
Ash Wednesday, 1956

CONTENTS

MAN IN THE MIDDLE

PROLOGUE

No sin—deadly or otherwise—would be involved in the decision to skip this Prologue, for the time being, and to begin at once the reading of the Trialogues.

Sin is an indigestible cake which can be sliced many ways. In the Middle Ages it was customary to slice it seven ways. Medieval theologians had the wit to see that the thousand and one (or ten thousand and one) sins of which men are capable can be traced back to, and deduced from, certain capital or root sins (*radices*—roots of sin), basic tendencies within every child of man as he comes from the womb of nature and is speedily warped by his environment. The Seven Sins are not themselves acts, but *logismoi* ("hidden motions of the soul") from which, singly or in combination, all manner of sinful acts arise. They are, in short, elements in the human character as we know it from our experience.

3

Unquestionably the number "seven" exercised a fascination for the medieval mind. Yet there is no magic in the number itself. As a matter of fact, some early catalogues list eight capital sins. There would be nothing to prevent an inventive thinker from extending the number to nine or ten, and perhaps an economical thinker could pare it down to six. Seven won out, however, not merely because of the mystic appeal of the number, but chiefly because the seven sins there specified come close to covering the ground and happen to be true to life. From these seven natural or acquired qualities can be derived, by permutation and commutation, most of the deviltry in which that excellent creature Man also, unfortunately, excels.

As a pedagogical device, The Seven Deadly Sins found their way into treatises on ascetical theology, handbooks for confessors, devotional addresses, morality plays, stained glass windows, and sculptured wood and stone. Not as anything more than a pedagogical device does it constitute the theme of this present book. The traditional names are retained but are translated into a corresponding number of thoroughly contemporary settings. Although a figure called JOHN appears in each of the trialogues, there has been no attempt at consistent characterization, since John, in accordance with our design, is not a particular person but is *Everyman*. (Accordingly, it must not perturb anyone that, for example, John in one trialogue is complete with wife and children, while in another trialogue he is a bachelor!)

"But the trialogues don't get anywhere." "There's no resolution of the conflict, no final answer, no clear defeat of the evil, no smashing victory for the good." These comments are typical of some of the reaction the trialogues received when they were presented in the Cathedral and over the air. This, too, was in accordance with our design. Well do the authors remember their disappointment on first making acquaintance with the dialogues of Plato. So much conversation, so much dialectic—and yet no clinching of the argument, no ringing affirmations, no total victories, and no abject capitulations. Yet all this was in accord with the Socratic method, the one which we, with inferior talent, have tried to follow. For our intention is neither to dictate answers nor to hand out pat solutions but to promote within the soul further debate in which each individual, rewording the questions to fit his own particular situation, will be led to seek his own answer to the great question. Hence, what is offered in these trialogues is not a sort of novel which one may sit back and enjoy, but a series of modern morality plays which demand of the hearer or reader maximum self-activity. While no one is to be begrudged whatever "entertainment" he can find in recognizing in John traits exhibited by his friends and associates, the real point is to look *through* John into one's own soul. John is everybody because he is nobody in particular. In other words, he is only a transparent medium for seeing certain aspects of universal and perennial problems.

The wisdom which led the Church to detect that particular sins have their root in seven capital sins also led the Church to discern that these seven, in their turn, spring from something deeper still: from *Sin*—from a false relationship to God. Expressed another way, six of the sins find their origin in the seventh: *Pride*—that is, man's tendency to be self-centered. In its root, Sin is man's attempt to live life where the wellspring of life is not. It is the arrogance which would get along without God, the presumption born of listening to the serpent's word: *Eritis sicut Deus!* For this reason, there has been appended to the trialogues on the Seven Deadly Sins an eighth trialogue on Original Sin.

Of this much misunderstood doctrine it will suffice, in the present context, to register our complete agreement with the Report of the Commission on Christian Doctrine appointed by the Archbishops of Canterbury and York in 1922 when it states: "What seems to be of practical importance in the conception of original sin may be summarized as follows: Man is by nature capable of communion with God, and only through such communion can he become what he was created to be. 'Original sin' stands for the fact that from a time apparently prior to any responsible act of choice man is lacking in this communion, and if left to his own resources and to the influence of his natural environment cannot attain to his destiny as a child of God." [1]

We should take our cue from the Bible, which refuses to waste much time and energy speculating about "how man got that way." Biblical realism eschews such speculation as something that easily degenerates into an ethical evasion of our present duties. It is idle to seek Adam in the dim mists of antiquity when it is our own house that is on fire. Christian anthropology insists only that man—each and every man—was created by God, for fellowship with God,

[1] Temple et al., *Doctrine in the Church of England* (New York: The Macmillan Company, 1938), p. 64. Quoted with the permission of the publisher.

and yet actually is in flight from God, trying to separate himself from God. The heart of man turned in upon itself: there lies the heart of the problem. And the problem finds a solution only when God, by the infinite strategies of love, succeeds in recapturing our hearts.

When, in this emphatic use of the word Sin, man is accused by the Church of being a sinner, he is not being berated for an isolated wicked deed or even for a whole succession of such deeds. The Church is concerned here, like a diagnostician, to track this disease to its source. For particular sins are symptoms, not causes, of man's malady. Perhaps the best brief way of stating the case is: Because man is sinful, he sins. It has, therefore, been suggested that Sin is a word which properly has no plural.

Yes and no.

When a child thinks of Sin, he thinks of specific naughty acts. He reckons as follows: Last Tuesday I was naughty because I did this or that; then three days went by in which I was a good boy; but on Saturday I was naughty again, and again late Sunday afternoon; let's see—that makes three sins in all; not so good as last week's performance but better than the week before that. Childishness, as someone has remarked, always sticks to the numerical. When spirituality has matured a bit, it begins to understand that in addition to these sins of commission there are other types of sin, just as bad if not worse, called sins of omission. It is not only that we've done things we ought not to have done but that we've also left undone some things we ought to have done. There has been neglect of duty, failure to utilize opportunities. These failures are now tallied and added to the record. This marks an advance in perception, but it is still confined to the quantitative area.

But now, maturity. The spiritually mature man gradually perceives that the sins present to his consciousness represent more than isolated spiritual defeats. Somehow they are all connected. From his mistakes, his slips, his occasional misdeeds, he comes to understand the deeper malady: that sin is an unfathomable continuity. His peccadilloes, though they do not exactly shatter the world, bring the deeper malady to light. They are the little symptomatic mistakes which exhibit his distance from God. For such a man confession is far more than a mere enumeration of particular sins; it is an understanding, before God, of the continuity of sin in itself.

Now he makes the Sign of the Cross over himself and is ready for the deep plunge: from the *quantitative* to the *qualitative*, from "We have left undone those things which we ought to have done; And we have done those things which we ought not to have done" to "And there is no health in us." The very fact that one can say this with utter sincerity argues, of course, that there is some health after all; but this health, like the courage it takes to make so honest a confession, comes from the fact that the confession is addressed to the God who absolves the sinner as soon as the sin is honestly faced and penitently confessed. Confession becomes possible when it is offered in faith as an act of obedience to the God who commands it. The courage to stop kidding ourselves and concealing from ourselves our true condition comes from definite convictions about God, the God who, as Archbishop Temple said, "must abolish all sinners; but He seeks to abolish sinners by winning them out of their sin into the loyalty and love of children in their Father's home." [2]

The first function of the doctrine of Original Sin, then, is to point to the fact that in each individual there is this underlying continuity, this condition, this status of alienation from God, which, so long as it goes unremedied, forms the inescapable background of all his actions, good and bad, and colors all that he does.

But the doctrine has a second function. It points to the continuity and cumulative power of sin in history. This second function is suggested by the synonyms by which Original Sin has been called, such as "inherited sin" and "racial sin." These synonyms are vulnerable to misunderstanding and have in fact been tragically misunderstood (some of the blame for which must be borne by a minority group of theologians), as if the Church thought that the procreation of children is itself an evil thing, for thereby sin is propagated. This error we repudiate in the words of Søren Kierkegaard: "Sinfulness is not an epidemic which is transmitted like cowpox." Despite the distortions sin has introduced into the realm of sex as into every other realm, we believe that the command of God is still "Be fruitful, and multiply"; and we regard the birth of every child as a divine creative act, an occasion for rejoicing. Nonetheless, should it surprise us, really, that our children come to resemble us in many matters that matter much? At the present stage of our

[2] William Temple, *Christus Veritas* (London: Macmillan and Co., 1924), p. 259. Quoted with permission of the publisher.

biological knowledge, it is impossible to affirm or deny the inheritance of acquired characteristics. We shall have to let this question rest until we have better information. But whether or not we inherit acquired characteristics biologically, we certainly come into a legacy left by them sociologically! Thus, although we have, in the birth of a child, a fresh divine creative act, this child is by birth introduced into human history—of which there's been a powerful lot, and much of it powerfully bad. The new beginning occurs, that is, within an old context. The child's environment goes to work on him from the very start, shaping him and misshaping him. There are good social influences, of course, as well as bad ones. But from the first flickers of consciousness, the child is under the influence of a thousand pressures, none of which he knows by name but all of which will have left their mark on him before he can even identify them by name. He imbibes them—almost with his mother's milk. In this sense, the child—though he comes untainted from the hand of God—falls heir (by the simple fact of being born and before he has made a single conscious choice) to standards and mores which, when he comes to choose, will largely have preconditioned him and dictated his choice.

The champions of freedom (and we humbly claim membership in their ranks) would do the cause extraordinary disservice if their zeal to defend freedom, and to insist on man's ethical responsibility, blinded them to the element of truth in the various deterministic accounts of human behavior. In assessing the degrees of responsibility and guilt, not only charity but simple accuracy force us to make due allowance for the fact that in some sense human beings are caught up in, and are swept along by, economic and social forces over which they have less than perfect control. Partly through their own fault and partly through the curious fatality of being alive in a world like this, people get entangled in the interlocking system of corporate sin and guilt and are thus propelled, by sin's own momentum, down dark ways they—left to themselves—might never have frequented. As someone has said, a new species of man, never intended by God, has sinned itself into existence.

So there is the phenomenon to which Original Sin points: the massive, pervasive historical drift and drive which determines with a kind of necessity or fatalism much of human behavior. Much of what the individual does is not his fault. It is fate. This is Sin, in the singular, with a capital S.

Yet the Bible detests vague generalities. In a highly embarrassing, almost impertinent way it lists particular sins and does not shrink from calling them by their rightful names, however indelicate. This means that the Bible continues, in spite of everything, to pay man the compliment of regarding him as free, responsible, and guilty, open to challenge and capable of response. But that is not all the Bible knows. Knowing man as well as it does, it knows that sinful men will be all too quick to grasp this doctrine and wrest it to their own damnation by seeking to skulk behind it. Man is seldom more disappointing than he is at this point. So eager is he to evade an unwelcome responsibility, and so tortured is he by his burden of guilt (both the actual guilt and the fictitious guilt a diseased imagination engenders), that he is not only prone, but positively keen, to find in "racial sin" an excuse for his own misbehavior. The alibis spring readily to his lips: "I couldn't help myself. You see, I was a dead-end kid; I was born on the wrong side of the tracks—or in Hitler's *Reich;* I didn't get enough vitamin C; it was all a matter of my glands; my father being what he was; the relations between my parents being strained," etc., etc. How convenient, in a way, to take refuge in a concept like "collective guilt" or "inherited sin." How comfortable to say a "general confession"—and let it go at that. "There's nothing we can do about it." This, of course, is new sin, the sin of denying one's personal complicity by the simple expedient of transferring it to the account of the entire human community, or eventually to God Himself, and so to waltz away scot-free. Strange freedom! The freedom afforded by declaring oneself not free.

This comfort and this convenience the Bible disallows, just as does the God who reveals Himself through the Bible. He employs every legitimate tactic to upset the easy security achieved by the moral coward's abdication of responsible selfhood. This is why, faced with the dictum that Sin is a word which properly has no plural, we have answered, *"Sic et non."* For there is yet a dialectic to be explored between sin and sins, fate and freedom, since biblical religion never permits itself the luxury of oversimplification. It is prevented, by the claims of truth, from attaining the neat logical statement which could be had either by blaming everything on fate or else by blaming everything on freedom. It insists, on the contrary, that human acts always result from a curious mingling of both destiny and decision, fate and fault; and it is humble enough to admit that it is quite unable to work out rationally an exact apportionment as to how much of human wrongdoing is due to the one or the other.

Here we see clearly Christianity's difference from, and affinity with, ancient Greek tragedy on the one hand, and modern ethical idealism on the other. It was the profundity of Greek tragedy to see that the tragic hero is in some sense "caught." Prior to the first utterance of his freedom is the epic background, a dark history of interlocking cause and effect. He is the descendant of an ill-starred race. Over him and his whole house presides a destiny, a fatality which largely predetermines him. Despite these circumstances and developments, however, he is not entirely passive, never merely a pawn. There still remains an element of freedom, and with this remaining freedom the tragic hero contributes to the tragedy of his house. If we demand to know whether he is guilty or not guilty, Greek tragedy returns the verdict: *ambiguous innocence.* In other words, by Greek reckoning, the accent falls more on fate than it does on freedom, although there is no denial of the fact that the tragic hero, while predisposed by fate, did actually contribute to the catastrophe and hence, in a limited way, is at fault. But the Greeks are compassionate: it was mostly fate; and we are not to judge the tragic hero harshly.

Modern tragedy, on the other hand, born of the Enlightenment and of nineteenth century optimism, tended to ignore the factors represented by the word *fate* and to concentrate almost exclusively on the element of freedom or responsible choice. Stringently ethical, modern tragedy has not the patience to listen to any epic background. It will hear nothing of the criminal's *vita ante acta* but sets him, as a solitary individual, in the dock and demands to know only what he was doing on the evening of April the twenty-ninth at precisely 11:35. Guilty or not guilty? If guilty, all guilt rests solely on the shoulders of the individual arraigned. This is the harshness of the modern, as contrasted with the mildness of the ancient, tragedies.

The curious religion called Christianity displays its strangeness precisely by accepting neither the Greek nor the modern solution. The Greeks said: Mostly fate, though partly freedom. Yesterday's moderns said: It's all freedom, it's his own fault. Christianity says: It's mostly freedom, though partly fate. Put another way: the verdict handed down by modern tragedy is either unambiguously guilty or unambiguously innocent; the verdict of the Greeks is, ambiguously innocent; the verdict of Christianity, ambiguously guilty. And by so saying, Christianity combines the wisdom of the ancients (expressed anciently by such concepts as *tyche, fortuna,* necessity, demon-possession, astral powers; expressed in our age variously by Marx with his economic determinism and by Freud and others with their differing theories of psychological determinism) and the wisdom of the ethical idealists (man is, in spite of all ideological taint and psychosociological conditioning, never purely passive but also active, free, and responsible). All narrowly logical objections to the contrary notwithstanding, Christianity here ventures to embrace a paradox. In general, paradox is something to avoid. Often it is only a dodge, the refuge of lazy thinkers. Christianity resorts to paradox only in cases where the venturing of a paradox presents the sole possibility of retaining hold on two truths that are persistently discovered in human experience, however contradictory they may appear.

The doctrine of Original Sin, properly understood, does not whitewash man or provide a hiding place for ethical cowards. It does, however, seek to say what may be said to show that in the case of every sinner there are extenuating circumstances which plead in his defense and argue for clemency. Religiously understood, the doctrine is a tremendous consolation—for the religious man. But this is a *religious* consolation —and woe to the man who would use it as a shield to protect himself from the searching judgments of God! The truly religious man will face God with the admission, "I, and I alone, O Lord, am guilty of this sin." And when he thus personally takes full responsibility upon himself, then he will hear God saying: "Yes, my son, you are guilty; but not you alone. For this is a universal sin which has manifested itself also in thee." And he will be consoled. Unhappy the man who would appropriate this consolation without first having acknowledged that he, and he alone, is guilty!

In the long history of Christian thought the pendulum has swung constantly from a preoccupation with particular sins, on the one side, to absorption with man's sinfulness in general, on the other. The first attitude results in a superficial moralism that relies upon and appeals to man's self-taught faith in the possibility of his being master of his fate. With *divide et impera* as its motto, it naively assumes that particular faults can, one by one, be rooted out by individual moral endeavor (and, in modern times, that social evils can be subdued by setting up a sufficient number of committees). We need not labor the point that first pride and then disillusionment have been the fruitage of this approach. This very disillusion always leads, in turn, to the opposite error. Oppressed by the massiveness and interlocking structure of sin, men have despaired of the possibility of dealing with particular sins and thus have neglected the little bit of the task that could be undertaken now, today, this very moment, with God's help. Quite as N. H. Søe has put it: "If the fact of Sin be neglected, we easily get mere moralism; if, at the opposite pole, sins be neglected, we easily end with the complacent acknowledgment that we all are just 'miserable sinners'; the personal sting is withdrawn, and the fight against particular sins, into which God by His Spirit would lead us, is neglected."

Evidently, the task is to learn from our sins that there is such a thing as Sin, yet never—in despair over Sin—to lose sight of the sins or lessen the campaign against them. The task, in sum, is to see in sins our Sin, and in Sin our sins; but above all, to see standing behind it all, the God who troubles the conscience in order to remind us that He is not only Judge but also the Friend of sinners.

Real battles are waged within the conscience of man every livelong day. Christianity's explanation is simple: though sin is self-willed separation from God, in the enterprise of separating himself from God man can never succeed. Ontologically, by virtue of his created being, man is bound to the God from whom he would flee. To speak of sin as separation, as is the fashion of the day, is, therefore, incomplete. It would be more nearly accurate to say that sin is a false relationship to God, of man's own making; a dis-relationship which is nonetheless supported by a relationship. And where there is this dis-relationship supported nonetheless by a relationship, *there* there will be anxiety, unrest, and problems of conscience.

These themselves are now the indices, albeit negative ones, of man's greatness. Only a creature as great as man could make himself as miserable. In the greatness of man lies the gravity of his guilt; in the greatness of God, who makes man great, lies the possibility of man's redemption.

i
WRATH

Outwardly calm but inwardly seething, John returns to his desk after having been hauled on the carpet by his boss, when—up pops the Devil!

TEMPTER: Well, I see the boss blew up at you again today, John. You're probably not calmed down from it yet.

JOHN: Calmed down? I never got worked up. You ought to know me well enough to know that I never let him faze me.

VOICE: It would be interesting to know, John, just how you handle the boss's outbursts of temper without retaliating in kind.

JOHN: I'm too smart to do that.

TEMPTER: You mean you just take it?

JOHN: Oh, no! I haven't forgotten a single instance. He doesn't know that there's any aftermath; but I am quietly gathering the data to undermine him. Every time he flies off the handle, he un-wittingly gives me material for my files—more leads for the case I'm building up against him.

VOICE: But what can you do to him, John? After all, he's the boss.

JOHN: Never you mind. I have my ways. I've been cultivating some of the directors and flattering them that they have through me an inside chan-nel into the inner workings of the firm. That re-lationship gives me a chance to drop hints, now and then, which cumulatively are laying a foun-dation of distrust and suspicion that will stand me in good stead when my time comes. And when it does, the boss will never know what hit him.

VOICE: John, I accuse you; I accuse you of the sin of wrath.

JOHN: How absurd!

TEMPTER: How absurd indeed! I've never heard a man deal with a problem in a more calm and col-lected—

VOICE: Collected? Or calculated?

JOHN: It doesn't matter. Wrath means getting angry. At that my boss excels, but my reactions are just the opposite.

TEMPTER: I can vouch for that. I've had a good influ-ence on John in this regard. I've taught him to hold his tongue and to check his temper.

VOICE: You pious fraud! You know exactly what you're doing. But since John doesn't, I'll try to clear up one point. There is an explosive kind of wrath which expresses itself in a hot show of temper. But the essence of wrath is not heat but hate. The man who flares up, with flushed face, and torrid outburst—

JOHN: That's my boss!

VOICE: Often such a man does not necessarily harbor hate and nourish grudges.

TEMPTER: Oh, I think your boss does that, too.

VOICE: Does he really, John?

JOHN: I'm not quite sure.

VOICE: You think he's keeping a dossier of all these instances to use against you?

JOHN: I don't think he's smart enough to do that.

VOICE: Or not hateful enough?

JOHN: So you're really absolving that hothead!

VOICE: Now get me straight: his choleric disposition does not greatly recommend itself. He is an example of wrath in the primary sense of the word. An irate man, his tantrums damage him and hurt others.

TEMPTER: Wait! You're making too blanket a judgment on another of my clients. His bold reactions have helped some people to see the error of their ways—

VOICE: I'm sure that you have comforted him with that thought.

JOHN: I'm sure, too. The boss said to me the other day after he had thoroughly blessed out one of the secretaries: "I certainly gave her a piece of my mind; but it will do her a world of good."

TEMPTER: Maybe it did.

JOHN: Yes, it got her started looking for a better job!

TEMPTER: But back to the boss—

VOICE: Yes, as far as the boss is concerned, his comment about the "good" his outburst achieved was just a rationalization intended to make him feel better about what he did and to make you not feel so bad about him. Any such outburst is really humiliating to the person guilty of it as well as to the person at whom it is directed; and a man hates to admit he's wrong.

JOHN: Well then, you oughtn't to be so hard on me and so light on him.

VOICE: It's *you* we're talking about now—you with your cold anger. But have no fear, I've been planning to lay down the law to him.

TEMPTER: I'd like to join you in the session.

VOICE: If you don't mind, I think I'd do better without you. Anyway, my point to John is that his anger is as cool as the boss's is hot.

TEMPTER: When you put it that way, I'm prepared to defend both kinds of wrath.

VOICE: Defend on!

TEMPTER: You're behind on your psychology. When a man feels aggrieved, he has to react somehow; and if he suppresses his sense of grievance, it's unhealthy.

VOICE: I know your deep concern for everyone's health and welfare.

TEMPTER: No sarcasm here! This is a serious matter. The slang phrase "burned up" is actually a scientific description. When the lid is put on top of an antagonistic emotion, the smothered fire wreaks its vengeance in the man's depths. He may think it's put out; but it smoulders and smoulders, and has a searing effect on the unconscious mind.

VOICE: That's more truth than I've heard you speak in a long time.

TEMPTER: So it's far better for a man not to inhibit himself. His retaliatory instincts were implanted in him by nature. They've got to have their play.

VOICE: Yes, but it's a question of what kind of play.

To bottle up wrath is to destroy the self. To unleash it is to destroy others. But I submit that there is another way. If a catalytic agent can be introduced, the steam generated by wrath can be a power of healing. In other words, let there be action rather than suppression, but let it be constructive action.

JOHN: What's this catalyst you're talking about?

TEMPTER: Nature does not supply it.

VOICE: No, it doesn't. Where it comes from—we'll come back to that. But first let me give you an example of it in action. Suppose a married man has been unfaithful to his wife. His experiment in independence soon shows itself for what it is: a sordid, empty affair. He wants to be reconciled to his wife. But he realizes now that he's done more than break one of the Ten Commandments. He's broken his wife's heart. And what can he expect from her now but wrath—her indignation, her righteous abhorrence of him and of what he's done?

JOHN: I doubt if that was her reaction. I would think rather that, threatened by a rival, her love for him would have been quickened, her possessiveness heightened.

VOICE: Yes, at first, to be sure. But as the affair dragged on, with the help of our friend here, her love turned to hate, her possessiveness to rejection, her ardor to wrath.

TEMPTER: In that sort of situation, I would counsel the customary peace offerings: two dozen American Beauty roses and a box of chocolates. And if they won't do the trick, he can always mortgage something and resort to a mink coat.

JOHN: Oh, don't be so flip! Obviously we're hearing about a real woman, a woman with standards, who has really been hurt.

VOICE: Yes, hurt. And unless the man's a fool, he'll be quick to see that there's nothing he can give her, nothing that he possesses, which will entitle him to be admitted again to her good graces. His wife has every right to go to law against him—read him out of her life. But now, what if she could find it in her heart to absorb the hurt of his misconduct and transmute this whole tragedy into an expression of her love? What if, without recriminations (she sees that he's been sobered by the experience) and without patronizing or putting herself on a pedestal above him, she takes him to herself?

TEMPTER: She's simply suppressing her wrath.

JOHN: No, she's sublimating it.

VOICE: Sublimating it—in the real meaning of that word, she's making it sublime. Her having undergone suffering and overcome bitterness toward it, is the catalyst I was talking about.

TEMPTER: The ladies I'm closest to aren't capable of that.

VOICE: The ones who stay closer to me are.

TEMPTER: What have you got that I haven't got?

VOICE: I have behind me a God who behaves this way. Not just this way, of course. The analogy of the forgiving wife isn't entirely perfect. Her love changes for a season to hate and then back to a deeper love; whereas in God, His judgment on evil and His love for the evildoer both remain constant.

JOHN: But what does God's being that way have to

do with the action of the wife in your story?

VOICE: This: a wife is more likely to react forgivingly if she knows that over and over again she has been forgiven in precisely that way by the One to whom she is ultimately responsible: namely, the living God. For her, forgiveness of the husband is at a price. She suffered, as she took up the hurt. And, in a way that we don't fully understand, this is true of God, too. Such a God is revealed in the Old Testament—for example, in the Book of Hosea—and in the Cross of Jesus Christ. In human forgiveness and in divine forgiveness alike, *without the shedding of blood there is no remission of sin*—as Scripture says.

JOHN: You've got a long way to go with me on all this, but I can see how, if you are dealing with somebody who really wanted to be forgiven—

TEMPTER: But your boss has never asked to be forgiven.

JOHN: That's for sure; so none of this applies to me.

VOICE: You say that only because I've yet to get to an important point. You see, the wife in my illustration, if her love were great, could have made clear to the husband, even before he repented, that she, although taking the hurt, was ready to forgive him.

TEMPTER: That's pretty much beyond the capacity of a wife.

VOICE: Perhaps; but not beyond the capacity of God. Hosea brought back his errant wife who had played the harlot and had reached the ignominy of being sold on the slave market—and he did this before he had a chance to inquire of her state of mind toward her sins or toward him. And as to the Cross, St. Paul tells us that *while we were yet sinners, Christ died for us.*

TEMPTER: I know some theology, too, and—

VOICE: Yes, one on my side has observed the same. James is credited with having said, *Also the devils believe and tremble.*

TEMPTER: Let's keep personalities out of this. I was merely about to say that even God doesn't forgive the sinner until he wants to be forgiven.

VOICE: But the important thing is: God has made clear that His forgiveness is always ready, always available, just as in the Parable of the Prodigal Son—which I trust you know, since you spent some time with said son or his counterparts. In the parable, the father ran to meet the returning son when he was yet afar off—

TEMPTER: John's boss is afar off all right!

JOHN: That's the truth! Never a word of apology. The same old pattern repeated over and over again: abuse followed by silence.

TEMPTER: And so, Mr. Fixit, what would you suggest that John do?

VOICE: How you read my thoughts! A suggestion was on the tip of my tongue: *take the initiative.* John, have you ever used your fertile imagination to think up—after one of these scenes—some especially thoughtful word or helpful act?

TEMPTER: That's bootlicking.

VOICE: It could be—depending on John's motive. But he could turn all this energy he's been putting into trying to "get" his boss into trying to help him.

JOHN: But how do I know that this will get the boss off his high horse?

VOICE: You don't know. You risk it, just as God does.

JOHN: I think I see—

TEMPTER: No you don't! You don't know the Bible as well as I do—

VOICE: Yes, John, the Devil can quote Scripture.

TEMPTER: The Bible says that Jesus fashioned a whip of cords and drove the money-changers out of the temple.

JOHN: Oh, I know that passage. I've made it practically the motto of our League for Pure Government up in Floral Gardens. And, if I may say so, I'm the founder and president of the movement. We're incensed over the deepening corruption and mounting taxes of the city government given us by the Coordinationist Party, and we've got to drive the rascals out.

TEMPTER: That sounds estimable.

VOICE: His support ought to make you suspicious, John. You see, if the politicians you are trying to oust are really all that bad, then he's for them more than for you.

JOHN: Oh, I know he's for them, all right. Everything they've done has been inspired by the Devil. That's why I hate them so.

VOICE: Here it is obvious that our demonic companion is playing both sides of the street. He's made you hate them.

TEMPTER: Why shouldn't I?

VOICE: Because we're not supposed to hate anybody.

JOHN: Not evildoers?

VOICE: Not evildoers. You should hate the evil that

they do, but you mustn't hate the people. Jesus said, *Love your enemies.*

TEMPTER: Maybe John can and maybe he can't. But I don't see what difference that makes as to how he acts. You, of all people, would agree that citizens should take steps to oust a bad government.

VOICE: You've got me right there. But it does make a great deal of difference as to what goes on in John's heart and mind. Hatred of evil is good for a man and for his relations with God—because God more than anyone else hates evil; hatred of people, however, sears a man's soul and separates him from God—because God goes on loving even bad people.

JOHN: What practical difference does that make? I'd still go on fighting them.

VOICE: It even makes a practical difference. Hatred directed towards persons blinds one to the facts; one attributes evil motivation to everything that is done, whether in itself a particular action is good or bad, wise or unwise. The result is name calling and blanket denunciations. Hatred really makes a man a poor fighter because it partly blinds him to the target. Of hatred fanaticism is born.

TEMPTER: Well, then, let's have more such fanatics. They get things done.

VOICE: They get things done all right. The result is often destructive and conducive to lasting hatreds which can divide up the community rather than unify it.

JOHN: Then you think we should slow up our efforts, relax our zeal?

TEMPTER: That's what he wants you to do, John: become a regular Mr. Milquetoast in your town.

VOICE: Not at all. Work as hard as you can to bring the real issues and facts to the attention of the public and to replace the present officials with ones you think can do a better job. Still, I think you're a little naive to describe what you and your friends would achieve as "Pure Government"—

JOHN: Oh, that's just a name we chose.

VOICE: But labels like that all too well indicate—and encourage—the fanaticism which assumes that everything and everyone on the other side is 100 per cent evil and that you people are 100 per cent right and good.

TEMPTER: But isn't that the most effective way to keep up morale? Certainly in a war it's better to have our soldiers really hate the soldiers on the other side, really thirst to kill them.

JOHN: That's too much for me. I think you are underrating the positive idealism which has kept most of our soldiers going.

TEMPTER: Remember, you were in the infantry in the last war, and you were so good a killer you got a medal for it.

JOHN: I know; and I shudder every time I think of it. I had no hatred against those poor fellows we did away with in that machine-gun nest, and I wish they were alive today. But we had to do it.

TEMPTER: But if you weren't against them why did you do it?

JOHN: I wasn't against them. I was against their government and the threat to my country and to freedom which they represented.

Voice: Amen! And, as my enemy here has admitted, your effectiveness in doing the necessary job didn't seem to be impaired in the least. John, take a cue from that in your work for reform in your community—and then carry on with full steam.

ii
LUST

John has just lit his pipe and is settling down in a comfortable chair to spend a quiet evening at home, when—up pops the Devil!

TEMPTER: John, I don't think you've been having a very good time lately. You used to be quite a Don Juan. Now I think you've become an old prude. You're single and not too old yet—and the ladies like you, you know.

JOHN: I'm having a good enough time; it's just that—

VOICE: His conscience has been working on him, you see.

TEMPTER: I gathered as much. That's why I thought I'd better reopen the subject. It's just not natural that he should rule sex out of his life.

VOICE: Oh, I haven't told him to do that. I've told him that sex is a good thing.

TEMPTER: He didn't used to think so—and that was better for my side.

VOICE: What do you mean?

TEMPTER: Well, as long as he thought it was essentially evil—his parents were unwittingly in cahoots with me in getting that idea across—he was easier to tempt. He resented the fact that married people had a special license to do something bad; and, besides, the fact that he thought it was basically unclean somehow added an extra piquancy to the attraction to it.

JOHN: You can say that again!

VOICE: That's why once when the tempter wasn't around I talked this all out with you, John. Do you remember?

JOHN: I do. You said sex is a good and beautiful thing God intended for our joy and fulfillment. In fact, you said it is sacramental.

TEMPTER: Sacramental?

JOHN: I had always thought that sacraments were something that go on in church.

VOICE: Strictly speaking, yes; but there are many relationships in life which have a sacramental character. For example, a handclasp, sincerely meant—not just one of a series of handshakes in a reception line—is sacramental; that is, it is an outward and visible sign of an inward and spiritual bond. And more than that, the outward sign helps make the inward fact—just as the sharing of bread and wine does in Holy Communion.

JOHN: Well, now I see why in the case of sex I shouldn't use the outward and visible sign unless there is an inward and spiritual side.

TEMPTER: Oh, there's always some inward side to it —friendship, respect, or at least common appreciation of *joie de vivre*.

JOHN: But is that enough?

VOICE: The inward and spiritual side God intended is the total and permanent pooling of lives, of hopes and fears, of strength and weakness.

TEMPTER: That pretty much limits it to marriage.

JOHN: Right. So now you have the answer to your question about what you call my prudish behavior—and this conversation is over, my demonic friend.

TEMPTER: By no means! I want you to hear me out, for your own advantage. The fact is, you're *not* married.

JOHN: So?

TEMPTER: Well, you're not getting any younger and you might as well enjoy yourself. For example, there is Rose. She adores you, and frankly she has made it pretty evident—I coached her a bit— that she wouldn't be stuffy about a gracious overture.

JOHN: I think maybe you're right. The thought has crossed my mind—

VOICE: You can credit him with that.

TEMPTER: Yes, you can—and I'm looking out for his best interests, while you're just worried about—

VOICE: His salvation.

TEMPTER: I'm talking about *now*.

VOICE: I mean *now;* his best fulfillment now.

JOHN: But I'm thinking about Rose—and it's a pleasant thought. I'm having dinner and going to a show with her tonight, as a matter of fact. I think this time I will accept her usual invitation to drop up to her apartment for a nightcap.

TEMPTER: Now, that's the old John I used to know.

VOICE: Yes, the old John. Remember Mary—a couple of years ago?

JOHN: Yes, all too well. She got hurt pretty badly—because I didn't really love her—

VOICE: But you pretended you did.

TEMPTER: But that's just where Rose is different. She's told John—I put this idea in her head—that she isn't serious, but would just like to be friends.

VOICE: My familiar adversary, are you still using that line? John, she may say that—may even mean it—but the fact is, if you go ahead, she or you or both may get more deeply involved than you realize, and then—

TEMPTER: Well, what's to keep them from getting married? It may turn out beautifully.

VOICE: You talk as though you really like happy endings!

JOHN: And I suppose there's always the risk that one might care more than the other—

VOICE: Or that even if both seem to care, one will be anxious—underneath, if not consciously. And this very mistrust of the devotion of the other may interfere with the stability of the relationship, may tear apart what might have been an abiding union—to the lasting hurt of one or both.

JOHN: But that wouldn't seem to apply to a more casual arrangement, say, with what we might call a "professional."

VOICE: No, that doesn't apply; but there are other

reasons why this thought—for which I can credit my opposite number here—is a bad one, too.

TEMPTER: Certainly such a girl is not going to feel hurt if her partner is not in love with her.

VOICE: True. But the hurt to her from the whole succession of relationships is profound. She is literally being "used"—and almost the basic ethical wrong is to use a person as a thing.

TEMPTER: But John's restraint in that regard isn't going to change her daily work.

VOICE: Maybe not; but her mode of life is due to x number of particular men, and each has a share in the moral responsibility for her degradation.

TEMPTER: But that's the crux of the matter: what's degrading or immoral about it?

JOHN: It's honest, at least.

VOICE: Honesty is not the only virtue. Here, what is a sacrament is being used sacrilegiously. The outward and visible sign is being used for its own sake—when there is no vestige of the inward and spiritual grace.

JOHN: So is it worse than an affair where there's affection?

VOICE: In one regard it is: it is more boldly sacrilegious.

TEMPTER: All he'd allow you is to think about it.

VOICE: No, I don't leave you that either, John.

TEMPTER: I can supply some interesting pictures for the mind.

JOHN: I know—

VOICE: Here our demonic companion is trying the old device known as "the camel's nose in the tent."

JOHN: I don't get you.

VOICE: It's a story that goes on and on. But in short:

one cold night on the desert the camel begs the Arab to let him put just the tip of his nose in the tent; it ends up, of course, with the camel in the tent and the Arab outside.

JOHN: What you mean is: first the fantasy, then the fact.

VOICE: Yes, and more than that. *Whosoever looketh on a woman to lust after her hath committed adultery with her already in his heart.*

TEMPTER: Certainly, John, such a notion doesn't appeal to you—a requirement of abstract purity even in the mind. What harm does thinking and imagining do?

VOICE: Action is founded on thinking and imagining.

TEMPTER: But he *won't* act: you have so inhibited him by your arguments.

VOICE: You, more than anyone else, know better than that. You're fully aware that what John will do depends on more than just the logic in his conscious mind. As we read in Proverbs, *Keep thy heart with all diligence; for out of it are the issues of life.*

JOHN: And just how does that apply here?

VOICE: John, when you ruminate about sex, dallying with the thought of it and doting on it, you are feeding your unconscious mind with fuel for the urges which can later flare up as compulsive acts.

TEMPTER: But, my conscientious foe, he still has your arguments to inhibit him.

JOHN: You bet! Every time you tempt me, his arguments give me quite a time.

VOICE: But what you, too, are overlooking, John, is the fact that the unconscious urges can set off a mechanism in the conscious mind which will produce counterarguments—even in neat syllogistic form—which in the moment of temptation may appear more plausible than the best basis of restraint I have supplied.

TEMPTER: Now wait a minute! You always try to pack his unconscious; you're always trying to get him to meditate—or worse still, to worship. I know the dangers: all this helps keep my suggestions from getting a hold on him.

VOICE: Not entirely. I may get him to spend an hour or so a week in worship and prayer, but during the rest of the time he is under quite contrary pressures from the world.

TEMPTER: Yes, John, have you read any good books lately, seen any good plays?

JOHN: Yes, a couple of plays. They both got pretty heavily into the subject of our discussion. I'm kind of embarrassed to admit that I enjoyed them.

TEMPTER: You needn't feel embarrassed admitting this in front of me, John. I don't share his opposition to the theater.

VOICE: Opposed to the theater? Not me! In fact I enjoyed one of those plays very much. I'm speaking of *Coffee and Compassion*. There was a lot of sex in it, and it was a first-rate play. The other play, however, that thing called *Fires of the Night,* I found 100 per cent offensive.

TEMPTER: How simple you are! The one you liked was the bolder—I might even say, the more vulgar of the two.

JOHN: I thought the same. *Fires of the Night,* I'll admit, had a lot of broad humor in it, but *Coffee and Compassion*—the play you liked—that really was frank to the nth degree.

VOICE: Look, I don't mind boldness. I don't mind realism. When the sexual aspects of a situation worth portraying are straightforwardly presented in order to illumine the actual shape of the human problem, then the spectator—with or without the aid of the playwright—has a genuine basis for grasping the dimension of judgment and redemption, and can be a richer person for the experience. This opportunity was certainly afforded by *Coffee and Compassion*.

JOHN: And as to *Fires of the Night*?

VOICE: Pornography.

TEMPTER: I object!

VOICE: No, I sensed you collaborated with the author; so you know very well what I mean. It was the deliberate parading of sex for the sake of sex. Its only purpose was to titillate.

JOHN: I will say for *Coffee and Compassion* that it made me feel I ought to give more attention to the possibility of marriage.

TEMPTER: If that sort of thing appeals to you, then at least your temptations will be over.

VOICE: May we hold you to that?

TEMPTER: Well, I wouldn't think of interfering with a happy marriage. But the marriage service does not include a ceremony of affixing blinders on the groom. An attractive girl is still an attractive girl.

VOICE: Right! I wouldn't want John to be blind to any of the beauty of God's creation.

TEMPTER: Well! You sound like you're on my side.

VOICE: Not on your life. If this fellow follows my lead, he will be loyal not because of an illusion that his wife is the only attractive woman God made—

JOHN: Perhaps I can be permitted that illusion for a few months.

VOICE: He will be loyal because he has made a decision —a decision to pool his life with this person and not with that person. It's a matter of commitment and vocation under God. And we will help him persevere in it.

TEMPTER: Oh, I could counter that. I suspect I could find some ladies of my acquaintance to intrude into the picture. You see, my righteous friend, you're being a bit old-fashioned. The monogamy you defend was no burden when the life expectancy was only thirty-five!

JOHN: I do suppose that after a while a married man fears he's missing something.

VOICE: He is. He is missing the frustration involved in a sexual relationship which has no abiding basis in anything profounder than sex; and what is gained by his very decision of restraint is a deepening of a relationship which over the years can be more wonderful than any telling of it.

TEMPTER: That's a very pretty way of putting what is just "lust legalized!"

JOHN: I'm sorry; it's too late in the conversation for you to get away with that. To me, lust means the wrong use of a thing which, when rightly used, is love.

VOICE: Good for you, John! But there's a half-truth hidden in what he's just said. It's a dolorous fact, but a spouse can use the marital partner for his own self-gratification. That is lust too—and not to be confused with love. The love I'm recommending, John, is the kind of love between husband and wife which appears only when the husband, knowing himself judged, forgiven, and loved by God, loves God in return; and the wife, knowing herself judged, forgiven, and loved by God, loves God in return, so that they judge, forgive, and love each other in, with, and through their mutual love of God. In other words, their marriage relationship is grounded in, and is a reflection of, their joint relationship to God.

JOHN: Let's see if I've got this straight. You're saying that a man, conscious of his faults before God and aware that God, though He judges those faults, forgives them and still loves that man—such a man will be better able to put up with his wife's faults, to be patient with her, and by his love for her help her to overcome them. And ditto for the wife, vice versa? Is that what you mean?

VOICE: Exactly.

JOHN: I think I'm getting the idea. Such a marriage would have something more to go on than mere physical attraction. The devotion of husband and wife to each other on the basis of physical attraction would be undergirded and safeguarded by their common devotion to God.

VOICE: And it isn't only a matter of one spouse managing the faults of the other and loving beyond them. A husband's gratitude to God and to his wife for this kind of love would increase his sensitivity to her special needs of fulfillment. Instead of simply "being himself" and "letting himself go," he will be consciously considerate of her needs of flesh and spirit. This, in turn, will constantly deepen his wife's love—physical and otherwise—for him.

JOHN: Sounds wonderful.

TEMPTER: Sounds very theological! I can see your adviser has no feeling for just plain romance.

VOICE: Theological it is—which is to say, God is in it. And God is no foe of romance! Indeed, He is its finest champion and defender, as He is also its Author. *Male and female created He them.* Far from excluding romance, the kind of love God would enkindle in His creatures is a love that gives romance a sure foundation and a constant source of renewal. Isn't that what you really want, John?

TEMPTER: Remember, John, it's a life sentence.

i i i
ENVY

After a hard day at the office and an unsatisfactory evening at home, John is trying to compose himself for sleep, when—up pops the Devil!

TEMPTER: I perceive you're burned up about something.

JOHN: You bet I'm burned up. And you'd be burned up, too, if you'd been through what I've been through today.

TEMPTER: Tough day at the office?

JOHN: Well, it began there. To the surprise of all of us, like a bolt out of the blue, they created an executive vice-presidency, and guess who got it?

VOICE: From the tone of your voice, obviously not you!

JOHN: Well, it wasn't anything I'd counted on. I had no stake in it. But it was a shock to find that Addison suddenly pops up as number two man.

41

VOICE: But you like Addison! I've often heard you say you admire him.

JOHN: Admire him? Of course, I admire him. Always have, still do. He's absolutely top-flight.

VOICE: Why so hot, then, little man? You've lost nothing. And another man's gained something. Can't you be glad that a lucky break has come his way?

JOHN: I don't begrudge his stroke of luck, but—

TEMPTER: One might wish that luck were a little more evenly distributed.

VOICE: The difficulty, I think, lies elsewhere: in the fact that John cannot bear to see another's prosperity if he can't share in it, too.

TEMPTER: And John's right. Admittedly, Addison is well qualified for the job, but John is every bit his equal in business ability.

JOHN: Oh, I wasn't looking for this job. Never entered my head that such a job would be available. But there are other good men in the company—Walters, for example.

VOICE: Would you have been any more pleased if Walters had got it?

JOHN: Well, maybe not.

VOICE: Isn't it a fact that you wouldn't want anyone to have it unless it were you?

TEMPTER: Watch it! He's trying to pin covetousness on you, John.

VOICE: No, not covetousness. Not this time. It's *envy*.

JOHN: Actually, I don't think it is. It's a perfectly natural resentment over the fact that Addison got the job because of connections. He came of a well-fixed family, went to the right schools, made the right fraternity, married the right girl, and moves in the right circles.

VOICE: Aha! I can see that your envy of him did not start only this morning.

TEMPTER: John, I know you well. You haven't coveted these things for yourself. And why should you? After all, you haven't had such a bad time of it. You came up the hard way and have made the most of your opportunities.

JOHN: Well, I guess I am what you call a self-made man.

VOICE: A self-made man who worships his maker, maybe? In any case, you've rather looked down your nose at Addison because he's not a self-made man in the sense you are.

JOHN: But that's because Addison just fell into one good break after another. He was born with a silver spoon in his mouth—everything has been handed to him on a silver platter ever since.

VOICE: If it's just a matter of good breaks, how can you blame him for it? The real question is: what has he made of the opportunities he's had?

JOHN: Oh, he's cultivated the arts, kept up on his reading, developed a wide circle of interesting friends. I've never had time for that sort of thing.

VOICE: Nor perhaps the liking or the ability?

TEMPTER: You're really running my client down!

VOICE: Not in the least. Addison had certain talents and has made the best of them. John had another set of talents and has made the best of them. The trouble I find with John is that he's unwilling to accept the fact that there are one-talent, two-talent, and five-talent men and that we get a different set of talents in each case. Everyone has different equipment; everyone has a different task. That's the way God has set things up—hence the individualism we all prize so much. The thing gets out of whack only when someone like you, John, isn't content to be the man he is and wants desperately to be the man he isn't.

JOHN: You mean, I want the credit for being a self-made man, and, at the same time, to be one who has had Addison's background and advantages?

VOICE: Yes, you want your particular talents and gifts —and his, too. You're a realist, John, and you know this just can't be. Your job is to be yourself; to be content that Addison is Addison; and to admire his gifts without being envious of them.

TEMPTER: Well, to change the subject, one thing Addison doesn't have is your wife.

JOHN: He certainly doesn't! And that's another thing. I came home early today, feeling as I did, and where is she? At a meeting of the Slum Prevention Committee.

VOICE: What's wrong with that?

JOHN: If it hadn't been that, it would have been a meeting of the Shakespeare Society; or else she'd have been at the museum looking at some of those silly modern paintings.

VOICE: But you must be pleased, John, that your wife manages your household so skillfully and that, on top of her duties as wife and housekeeper, she still has time for the many activities which mean so much to her.

JOHN: But I'm not interested in those things.

TEMPTER: I suppose you must feel, John, that with

her mind on these other things she doesn't enter enough into your concerns.

JOHN: No, I can't really say that. I have no complaints on that score; but I just can't get excited about all this culture and community activity.

VOICE: But that's all good in itself and important to her. What you're saying is: since these things are meaningless to you, you don't want her to profit from them either.

JOHN: Oh, I guess I don't mind—if that sort of thing appeals to her.

TEMPTER: That's reasonable enough. You go your way, she hers.

VOICE: Not so easy. A bit more than that is expected of you, John.

TEMPTER: Don't forget, he's footing the bills.

JOHN: I sure am. And what I'm not interested in I'm just not interested in.

VOICE: But, John, your wife has more needs than your money can supply. If she has a vivid interest, you can't leave her in the lurch. You've got to respond to it in some way.

TEMPTER: But you yourself said earlier that there is a variety of talent. John just doesn't happen to be made up the way his wife is.

JOHN: I don't like modern art; I don't like Shakespeare.

VOICE: You say that rather belligerently; but isn't there behind it a real sense of lack in your own make-up—a lack which you're unwilling to face, so that the things you lack in yourself you envy in another. Since you aren't like her, you demand that she be just like you.

TEMPTER: My competitor here—supposedly full of sweetness and light—is being pretty negative to-night.

JOHN: I've been feeling the same.

VOICE: No, as a matter of fact I have some positive suggestions.

TEMPTER: Watch out, John, he'll be trying to change you.

VOICE: Yes; and in these two ways: first, you can try—I might even say, for a starter, pretend—to be interested in the matters that have attracted your wife's interest.

TEMPTER: You will observe, John, that this is not a very honest suggestion. I hardly expected deception to be recommended from that quarter.

VOICE: I'm not talking about deception but about an honest effort to show interest. This showing of interest might well lead to an actual interest. For example, take modern art. A try might lead you, John, to the discovery that modern art has something to commend it, or it might even start you on the way to intelligent artistic criticism. There is gain for your marriage either way.

TEMPTER: You've gotten a long way from *envy*.

VOICE: I'm interested in getting as far away from it as possible, and I have shown John one way.

JOHN: You mentioned a second point.

VOICE: Yes, as to the instances where my first suggestion doesn't work—when you just can't get interested—you can admire your wife for the fact that she *can*.

TEMPTER: John, I have been thinking about the quite unsympathetic line which our foe has been taking on both of your problems today. I'm beginning to suspect that at heart he is an aristocrat. He wants you to keep in your place and be content that others have left you behind—and he wants you to take it, lying down. In exalting your wife's right to be what she is and Addison's right to be where he is, he obviously has no respect for your rights. I am a true democrat: everybody on a par, I say. This is justice and equality.

JOHN: You seem to be standing up for me, which is a comfort; but I don't quite follow you.

TEMPTER: My point is this. Equality is the ideal, and there's no reason why Addison should be on a pedestal above you; there's no reason why your wife should go out of her way to be something you cannot be.

VOICE: In other words, you think everything should be leveled down in every realm to the lowest common denominator. Now, I know something about our democratic ideals, too.

TEMPTER: Certainly justice and equality are fundamentals, sir!

VOICE: Here, true to his nature, the Devil is a liar. Democracy does mean equality of all persons before the law and, insofar as by law it can be provided, equality of opportunity—regardless of race or background. But these very things were not meant to put a ceiling on individual achievement.

TEMPTER: What were they meant for, then?

VOICE: They were meant to insure a framework within which each person can rise to whatever heights and attainments his own gifts and zeal can bring him—whether in business, the sciences, professional life, the arts, or athletics. To resent the fact that within this free framework different individuals reach different levels is *envy*.

TEMPTER: Really, I think you're making too much of this whole thing. What you call John's envy is simply a matter of his thoughts: he's been behaving all right.

JOHN: Yes, I reacted all right when I heard the news about Addison.

TEMPTER: What did you say to the others in the office?

JOHN: Oh, I said he's competent enough; he ought to do a fairly good job. I didn't have a thing to say against him.

VOICE: No, you just damned him with faint praise. What did you say about the job he has got?

JOHN: I said it wasn't too much of a job. I suggested that it may look better on paper than it will turn out to be in fact, and that Addison, behind his fancy desk, might find he's pretty much of a figurehead. I did remark that actually he won't have as much responsibility for the real work of the company as he had before, when he was down in the district office with us.

VOICE: I recall your saying something else, John.

JOHN: Well—yes, I did express my concern that maybe Addison was in fact being "kicked upstairs."

VOICE: What envy admires but can't have, it belittles. You're pretty good at that sort of thing, John. That's why you sneer at your wife's cultural and community interests. Secretly you respect them, but since you're not up to them, you debunk them. And before we drop this subject, I want to point out to the two of you that envy has quite opposite results in some cases. If a man thinks there's a good chance of working it, he seeks to imitate that which he envies.

JOHN: For example?

VOICE: John, that TV set you had installed last week—

TEMPTER: There's certainly nothing wrong with television.

VOICE: Not with TV but with the reasons why John moved so suddenly last week to get this set. May I remind you, John, what you said not less than two weeks ago?

JOHN: I remember—that I didn't enjoy TV in the least, and that I'd never have a set in the house.

TEMPTER: But he changed his mind.

VOICE: Yes, when his next door neighbor with some pride told him that he had bought a beautiful new set.

TEMPTER: That was just a little case of "keeping up with the Joneses."

VOICE: "Keeping up with the Joneses" is social climbing. An external thing you can readily buy with money. But it'll take more than having TV to keep up with that pair of Joneses. Once involved in that race, you'll find yourself alternating between copying them when you can and deriding them in chagrin when you can't: this is the mark of a snob.

JOHN: That's the last thing I ever thought anyone would call me! A snob is a superior person looking down his nose at an inferior.

VOICE: No, a snob is a person like yourself who has an exaggerated respect for social position and wealth, a person who is ashamed of himself for not having them, a person who wants them for himself—that's what makes him a social climber. And if he can't have them for himself, then his admiration turns to envy, and he changes his tune: that which he previously admired he now calls stupid, worthless, egghead. Envy, you see, is admiration gone sour. Envy derides what it desires because the lack of it makes one feel inferior—and that, envy cannot bear.

TEMPTER: John, our friend has done a very interesting job of pulling you apart. Just how, I wonder, would he go about putting you together again—even with all the king's horses and all the king's men.

VOICE: John, you have to start with the King and not with you. Back of all the particular circumstances that made you what you are stands God, who wanted you to be; and thus He stands behind you and is *for* you. With Him, you can venture to be yourself. Most people seem to have the notion that they must manage somehow to remodel themselves radically before God will have dealings with them, as if God sits and waits until certain specifications have been met. But the extraordinary thing is, God doesn't wait. He wants you just as you are.

JOHN: Just as I am? But I don't want to be just what I am all my life.

VOICE: Don't worry. There's not a chance that you'll stay just as you are. But that's where God, being a realist, starts; and that's where you have to start. He respects you for what you are, for the talents you have. He likes you better than you like yourself, sees more in you than you see in yourself. You have to catch up with what He already sees in you before you can move on, with Him, to be more than you now are. For this self is not a static, frozen thing but something dynamic and plastic, which can ever expand its tastes and capacities.

TEMPTER: But meanwhile it's pretty galling to see other people stealing the march on you.

VOICE: Other people's successes can serve us in many ways. That which is good in another and which you also find in yourself, you can respect and hold on to. That which is good in another and which you do *not* find in yourself, you can admire and emulate.

JOHN: I see where you're going. The next point is: Those qualities that you find in another but that you yourself lack, you can still respect.

TEMPTER: Precious little respect John has had from Addison!

VOICE: I think you're underrating Addison. But whether or no, my rather wide experience with the sons of men leads me to think that to the degree John begins to show respect for Addison's qualities, Addison will doubtless see more in John.

TEMPTER: And if Addison doesn't?

VOICE: John's assignment is clear. And if Addison lets me down, I will have to have a session with *him*.

TEMPTER: I'll be there!

iv

GLUTTONY

John has just returned from dinner with a friend at an exclusive restaurant and is preparing for bed, when—up pops the Devil!

TEMPTER: Your friend Buffington is quite a gourmet!

JOHN: A glutton I'd call him. All he thinks of is his stomach, and he's fifty pounds overweight. I keep myself trim—couldn't do it if I ate like him. I have my faults, but gluttony isn't one of them.

VOICE: You are taking a great deal of satisfaction in this innocence of yours, John.

TEMPTER: And he should. I think we can end this session right here.

JOHN: Good.

VOICE: Oh, I've hardly begun. I know you know, but I'm not sure that John understands what gluttony really is.

JOHN: It's eating too much.

VOICE: That's one expression of it; but I think we'll see what gluttony really means if we examine why overeating is wrong. Food's a good thing, you know. Gluttony is wrong because it is too much of a good thing at the expense of others. But to get back to your situation, John, you're pretty pre-occupied with the trimness of your figure, aren't you?

JOHN: Well, I watch what I eat and get plenty of good exercise.

VOICE: *Watch* what you eat! You insult more hostesses than any man I know, and your wife's kitchen activities are centered almost entirely around your calorie chart.

TEMPTER: Oh, he doesn't ask for much. He's satisfied with lean beef—

VOICE: Cooked just exactly medium rare—

TEMPTER: And a large green salad—

VOICE: With a specially prepared and tasty dressing.

JOHN: And don't forget my fruit compote—

VOICE: With different ingredients every night, and absolutely nothing to come out of a can: there might be a calorie or two left after the syrup is drained off.

TEMPTER: Don't listen to our sarcastic companion. You're right to take your diet seriously.

VOICE: Yes, he is—to take it seriously. But to be pre-occupied with it in a way that makes him the center of every meal at home and conspicuous at every meal away from home, is a subtle way of asserting the ego, and, more specifically, is actually a form of gluttony. And, as for your exercise—

TEMPTER: Don't let him talk you out of that, John. It's all very wholesome.

VOICE: John, do you know how many hours a week you spend tending to your physique?

JOHN: Oh, I go over to the gym after work for a workout and sometimes a swim; I play golf most of Saturday and go eighteen holes Sunday mornings if it doesn't rain.

TEMPTER: That sounds fine; it might do us good, too, don't you think?

VOICE: It might. But I don't have a wife and three young children. What are they doing all this time, John?

JOHN: Oh, I get home a little late from town; but I'm always there to kiss the kids good night and fool around with them for a while Sunday afternoon after I finish the Sunday paper.

VOICE: Principally the sports section—

JOHN: And my golf magazine.

TEMPTER: What's he trying to convict you of now?

VOICE: Simply gluttony again.

JOHN: But exercise is a good thing.

VOICE: Surely. But I remind you that gluttony is too much of a good thing, a preoccupation with one thing at the expense of others.

JOHN: I'm willing to go along with you that gluttony is more than just overeating, and I would get your point if I were doing something harmful like drinking too much. I'll grant that Mitchell is a glutton about liquor. I don't touch the stuff myself.

VOICE: Too many calories?

JOHN: No, I would say the less of a bad thing the better.

TEMPTER: He'll go along with you on that, John.

VOICE: As a matter of fact, I won't. I think the problem is precisely the same here as in the case of food. There can be too much of a good thing. The problem is again preoccupation, and I think that unless we see it in the same light as other forms of preoccupation, we're not going to help alcoholics very much. These damaging overemphases practically always reflect something deeper. They're used as an escape or a distraction from anxieties or unwanted responsibilities.

TEMPTER: Well, it's a hard world. Why shouldn't people have means of escape?

JOHN: It's made a harder world when they do. Mitchell just isn't on the job any more, and all the rest of us have to cover up for him.

VOICE: Just as your wife, John, has to take up the slack with the children when—

TEMPTER: John's a good father; but he thinks he'll be a better one, if fit and in good shape.

VOICE: John, they need *you,* not just your fitness—and so does your wife.

TEMPTER: You may be spending a little too much time in your exercise and sport, but it's not an escape for you; you're not hiding from anything.

VOICE: No? Let's face it, John. You've never been very comfortable in your relations with people—not even with your wife and children. This very worthy object of maintaining yourself as a physical specimen gives you a sense of significance that you don't feel in the office or at home.

TEMPTER: Well, isn't it just as well that he has that? John, he's really trying to knock the props out from under you.

VOICE: No, I'm trying to have you let up on an opiate long enough to see what your real trouble is. John, be honest with me. Don't you think that you really would have been trying harder to enjoy people and to enter into things at home if you weren't protected from doing so by this great concern for your physical well-being?

TEMPTER: It's kept him out of mischief. Physical culture is hardly a vice.

VOICE: And so, looking at men with other types of escape-mechanisms, such as drinking or overeating or gambling, he has been able to say "Thank God I am not as these other men"—publicans and sinners.

JOHN: Oh, you're making it too complicated. It's just that I like exercise; and what I do with my time is my own business.

TEMPTER: I like that sign of independence in you, John.

VOICE: I like independence, too, but not that kind. It just so happens that what you do with your time is not your own business. All your talents, all your energies, all your resources, all your time belong to God.

TEMPTER: But God doesn't supply any blueprints as to how it's all to be used.

VOICE: You do talk sense from time to time. It's true that God does not provide us with detailed instructions as to how to live. It's a high tribute He pays to the race of men that He allows each individual to be the manager of his own life.

JOHN: Then why don't you get off my back?

VOICE: Let me finish. You're a manager in the same

way that a district manager of your firm is. He has wide discretion as to how he goes about things, what priorities he gives at certain times to the various "lines" the company has, but he is responsible to the home office for an efficient and successful result.

JOHN: You mean he's "on his own" and yet *not* on his own.

TEMPTER: Well, then, that's a pretty phony kind of freedom.

VOICE: On the contrary. It's what gives human beings a dignity and a status in the universe. God has taken every man in as a partner in His great enterprise, giving him the freedom to work out the management of the particular area of life assigned to him; but like any senior partner God cares about what the junior partners do. If God didn't care what we do, our lives would be meaningless; if He directed every single step, our lives would be meaningless, too.

TEMPTER: That's all very pretty, John, but what it comes down to is that he doesn't want you to have any fun. And all work and no play makes Jack (if I may call you that) a dull boy.

JOHN: Yes, I work hard all day to support my family, and when I'm through I'm entitled to—

VOICE: Strictly speaking, you're *entitled* to nothing; God holds the title to everything. You're His steward, and He has entrusted these things to you. But you get God wrong if you think that He begrudges you any fun. He rejoices in your joy.

TEMPTER: What's your evidence for that?

VOICE: The fact that He created so many joyful things.

JOHN: Like that Latin myth about Hades: lots of tasty food around, but you can't touch it.

TEMPTER: Now you're thinking for yourself, John.

VOICE: But not very profoundly. God wants you to have more joy than you're having, John, not less.

JOHN: But my chief joy is in sport and exercise.

TEMPTER: And John is the best judge of what he enjoys.

VOICE: Not necessarily. He thinks he enjoys that most; but in proclaiming its joy he has a rather flat joyless tone. His very intensity about it suggests what was my earlier point: he is using it as a dodge, a time-filler, an escape from facing up to human relationships, which if he really entered aright would bring him a much deeper kind of joy and would bring out levels of his personal capacity now submerged.

JOHN: But I would hate to give up my regular forms of recreation.

VOICE: Distracted by this other fellow in our three-some, you obviously haven't been listening very carefully, John. There's no need at all for you to give up your gym work or your golf. What you need is something you already know about from your business: a time-inventory, so that you can best make up your mind how to distribute your time and energy among the various fruitful things you can do in the course of a week.

TEMPTER: He's trying to confuse your ethics, John. The safest, most straightforward kind of ethics labels some things as bad and some things as good.

JOHN: That's the kind of morals I was raised on, too.

VOICE: And that's the very kind that has misled you.

So you see Buffington's conduct is bad because it's neatly labeled gluttony, and you see Mitchell's conduct is bad because you've been taught that any alcohol is bad and drinking a lot of it is worse. But your approach, which labels exercise as good and wholesome, has hidden from you the fact that your own preoccupation with it has distorted your life, helped you dodge your real problems of human responsiveness. A clearer-headed running of your life will come from regarding none of the gifts or potentialities of creation as bad in themselves, and accepting the responsibility for limiting your use of these various possibilities in the light of your particular vocation under God.

JOHN: I'm beginning to see how this applies to me—and perhaps to Buffington, with his overeating. But it's too sweeping a generalization to apply to an alcoholic like Mitchell. *No* alcohol is good for him. One drink and he's off.

TEMPTER: That's the Achilles' heel of your system, my angelic friend!

VOICE: Not so fast. I know his case. In this period of his life, and perhaps for his whole lifetime, Mitchell's psychological—maybe even his biological—setup is such that, as John has said, *no* alcohol—even so much as a glass of sherry—is good for him. This is entirely apart from whether such refreshments are bad in themselves, a question on which good people can reasonably disagree. My point is that in his circumstances, Mitchell should as a matter of vocation eliminate from his life the use of this particular fruit of God's and men's creation, in order that he may best serve totally, just as other men must eliminate other things. For example, some gymnastics may be good for you, John, but not for a cardiac case.

TEMPTER:But there's nothing wrong with your heart, John, and our companion in the course of making such heavy weather over your innocent diversions has tried to take away your neat black-and-white sense of what is right and wrong, and all he's given you in its place is a fuzzy word like "vocation."

JOHN: That's what I was thinking myself.

VOICE: Not entirely by yourself. He helped you think that up. The Devil loves his clients to have a neat pattern of ethics which enables them to exclude their own conduct and attitudes from the area of "bad" and to avoid the weightier question of the proportion of their lives. So you can condemn gluttony in others when you see it in the literal form of overeating or overdrinking, but you feel quite satisfied with yourself in an overindulgence which has been throwing your whole life out of balance. Do you remember the story of David and Nathan?

JOHN: Vaguely.

TEMPTER: Bathsheba was in the plot.

JOHN: Oh, yes, I remember a movie about that. David found a way to get Bathsheba away from her husband—I think it was by ordering him into a precarious position in the front lines in a battle. Then Nathan told David the story of a rich man who took away the only lamb of a poor neighbor —and David at first didn't get the point of the story.

Voice: More than that. He expressed "righteous indignation" about the rich man's wrongdoing. And
it took these words from the prophet Nathan to
wake him up to the point: *Thou art the man!*
Tempter: And what's this got to do with John?
John: I get the point.
Tempter: I fear you do.

v

COVETOUSNESS

John is feeling quite pleased with himself as he heads toward home from the office, when—up pops the Devil!

TEMPTER: John, that's a nice thing you did for your bookkeeper Jenkins—taking care of the whole cost of his wife's operation out of your own pocket.

JOHN: Oh, the chance to do things like that makes life worth while.

TEMPTER: And Jenkins will always be indebted to you.

VOICE: John's hardly in any danger of forgetting that.

TEMPTER: There you go again trying to attribute an evil motive to what I should think is a victory for your side.

JOHN: I'm not perfect, but I seriously consider the obligations incumbent upon a man with a little means.

VOICE: Let's go back a step. You struggled hard to get

in hand what you so modestly call "a little means."

TEMPTER: Watch out, John. He is aiming to accuse you of covetousness. But he has the wrong man this time, hasn't he?

JOHN: I think he has.

TEMPTER: John works hard to make money. He certainly fulfills the biblical injunction *Be not slothful in business.*

VOICE: John, be on your guard whenever the Devil quotes Scripture.

TEMPTER: I suppose you'd prefer the text from the Book of Acts: *They had all things in common.* I can tell from your tone you're a foe of our free enterprise system. I suspect that you may even be a communist—

VOICE: I don't think it's necessary for me to answer that—

TEMPTER: And a Fifth Amendment communist! With this I can certainly discredit you with John and his crowd.

VOICE: No, I have no particular sympathy for those who will not state the facts about themselves. But the question of communism versus free enterprise is not relevant here.

JOHN: And why not? It is always the foremost question, sir.

TEMPTER: How successful I have been in selling that idea on both sides of the Iron Curtain!

VOICE: It is an important question, but not *the* question now, because our devious friend here is so flexible that he succeeds in nourishing covetousness in both soviet man and capitalist man alike. The Devil, like God, is no respecter of persons— or of economic systems.

TEMPTER: Let's get back to John. He's not interested in money, only in what money can buy.

VOICE: *Very* original! As if that weren't what everybody wants money for.

TEMPTER: *Touché!* But what saves John from covetousness is something that you, my fine-feathered friend, are always exhorting people to be: he is charitable, he is a steward of what he possesses.

JOHN: I will say that the important thing to me is the good I can do—the good I can do for people—with the money I've earned.

TEMPTER: His good works prove that. I think I've been following his activities more closely than you have.

VOICE: I think that's pretty evident! But I'm not unaware of his generous gifts to charitable institutions and to individuals in need.

TEMPTER: So you can see, his pattern is the exact opposite of covetousness. The covetous man strives to gain, so that he can have things. But this client of mine strives to gain, that he can give things away—that is, not to have things.

VOICE: In so picturing your client, I can see that you've taken a leaf from St. Paul who said, *Let him labour . . . that he may have to give to him that needeth.*

TEMPTER: St. Paul, is it? I've never counted him as on my side, but I'm glad we agree on this.

VOICE: Well, he is on *my* side, and I would ask you to notice carefully that the purpose of the striving and the acquiring is to give aid to others.

JOHN: I don't get your point, because that's exactly what I'm after.

VOICE: That's true; but in your case it is a means to something else you want more.

TEMPTER: There's nothing I can imagine John wants more than to help people.

VOICE: Your imagination doesn't usually need stimulating, but I'll try to help you. I don't want to be censorious, but could it just be that John's ego thrives on having others dependent upon him, indebted to him?

TEMPTER: You have an evil mind, distorting obviously unselfish motives. And you're talking in generalities. What single bit of objective evidence do you have for such an inference?

JOHN: Yes, what?

VOICE: Well, take the strings you usually attach to your gifts. Do you remember that large gift last year to the Society for the Increase of Discipline for Children?

TEMPTER: I do. One of the finest things John ever did.

VOICE: Could be, but John exacted a price—a seat on the Board.

JOHN: Oh, but that was for the good of the cause; I was afraid they'd get out of hand. They needed a practical businessman, and I filled the bill.

VOICE: They apparently weren't so aware of needing you that you dared to risk letting them think of electing you.

TEMPTER: But that was an isolated instance—

VOICE: Another of your favorite ruses, Mr. Tempter; a minute ago you claimed I was speaking in abstract terms and demanded a particular illustration; but when I furnish an example, you help John dismiss it as an isolated instance. However, I'll give you another example. John, you were very generous with Dennis, your office boy, when he wanted to go to college.

JOHN: Well, I did all I could.

VOICE: Yes, did all you could to mold him in your own image—

JOHN: I just wanted to save Dennis from getting involved in a lot of nonsense like literature and philosophy. My idea was to get him to learn practical things—accounting, business methods—things I wish I'd known more about when I started out.

TEMPTER: Showed great consideration for the boy's interests, I say.

VOICE: Except for one thing: Dennis didn't *want* to be a businessman. He wanted to be a writer.

JOHN: Oh, he thought he did; but it was just his idea. I knew what was best for him—just as I knew what was best for Jenkins when he started to work for me. I convinced Dennis that writers don't make enough money. Well-trained businessmen do!

TEMPTER: And Dennis has gone along with it.

VOICE: Sure—because John's holding the whip; he's paying the bills.

JOHN: I sure am. But I don't get all this. I may be right—I may be wrong—about what Dennis ought to prepare for—or, for that matter, about the affairs of the society you mentioned. But I try to decide things in the light of the best interests of all.

TEMPTER: He obviously has good intentions.

VOICE: That's what your home base is paved with. Maybe good intentions about the decisions he himself makes; but John has no intention of letting anybody else make any decisions if he can help it.

JOHN: So you think all these things I've been doing with my money are just for power?

VOICE: No, not just that—

TEMPTER: Well, look who's growing generous!

VOICE: Often it's to gain kudos, to get favorable publicity, to be thought well of.

TEMPTER: John *is* well thought of—and should be.

VOICE: I don't begrudge him that. It's all a question of why he does what he does. You may recall the answer the college president gave to someone who asked why a certain butter-and-egg man was given a Doctor of Laws degree. He answered: "Because the man looks like a women's dormitory." Now it's fine when credit comes; and usually it will come. But to give *in order that*—

JOHN: I'm beginning to get it. Jesus said that those who give alms that men may see them do so, already have their reward.

TEMPTER: Now, John, don't cringe before this imperious fellow. You have a good reason for letting the public know. You don't care a fig for the publicity.

JOHN: That's right. I'm the type that's more comfortable out of the limelight. But our public relations man tells me that it's good for the charities, encourages others to give; and it's good community relations—shows that the company assumes its citizenship obligations—

TEMPTER: And what's good for your company is good for the public. For example, its prosperity enables you to give even more.

VOICE: All this may be, and in fact I have encouraged many along these lines. Indeed, my Boss believes in good public relations, too (we call it evangelism). But it all comes down to the question of motive: of what John wants most when he strives "to get to give," as you would put it. I've raised the question with John; and this is the very question you are always trying to hide from him.

JOHN: All right. I understand the real question—and really will ponder it. Are you finished? I've had enough for now.

TEMPTER: So have I.

VOICE: So have I—except for one point. You know, John, generous as you are, your own standard of living is hardly meager. In other words, you've never sacrificed a thing in planning your giving.

JOHN: I guess not.

TEMPTER: And why should you? He thinks sacrifice has some value in itself. Typical of his negative attitude toward life! He's always wanting people to give up things.

VOICE: Quite the contrary. I want people to enjoy things—all the people possible. This is why all people are called upon to sacrifice. Sacrifice for a purpose. I never urged sacrifice just for its own sake.

JOHN: I like the sound of that, but aren't you selling the Scripture short? There's a lot of talk in the Bible about fasting.

VOICE: There is. But as in everything else, the purpose is the important thing. We confine our appetites either that we may do more for someone else or that we may be trained in discipline and thus better serve both God and neighbor.

TEMPTER: But John does serve generously.

VOICE: The test isn't how much John does, but how much John could do.

JOHN: But how do I know how much? One could, I suppose, give up everything.

TEMPTER: There you've got him. He can't answer that question.

VOICE: No, I can't. Because it's the wrong question. And to a wrong question there is no right answer.

TEMPTER: Then what is the right question?

VOICE: You see, John asks how much he must give on the assumption that it all belongs to him. If you start out with the assumption that all belongs to God, the question is—

JOHN: I get it: if all belongs to God, the question is, how much should I keep for myself?

VOICE: Exactly.

TEMPTER: All right. I'll shift to that ground. But you must remember, John, that you're not alone. A monk may be able to—

JOHN: But I'm not a monk; and, now that you remind me, I realize that most of my largest outlays of cash have not been for myself but for my family.

VOICE: Three TV sets?

JOHN: You don't understand. I have my favorite programs; my wife has hers; and certainly I don't want to deny my children the opportunity of seeing their favorite show; and with only two sets—

TEMPTER: You'd really be inconvenienced.

VOICE: I can imagine. How about the newly enlarged dining room?

JOHN: It made no difference to me, I assure you; but

it has enabled my wife to entertain more graciously.

TEMPTER: This, you see, my rigorous companion, is service to others; and charity begins at home!

JOHN: That's how I figured.

VOICE: John, there are worse things than all this; but I don't want you to deceive yourself.

JOHN: How?

VOICE: All this is the extension of your ego. You work hard to get things—not for yourself as you say. But I'll pay you a compliment: you're a good family man. Yet you can't tell me that the things you provide for your family are not provisions for yourself. To covet things for one's family is no different from coveting them for one's self, for a family is simply the self writ large. I won't say how many television sets, how many cars, how large a dining room you should have. But I do charge you to bring all of this under judgment— with this searching question: how much of the assets of which you are steward should you be holding back—for you *and* your family?

TEMPTER: John, it's all right for him to talk this way, but it simply isn't human nature. A man's family judges him by what he provides for them, and in turn the community judges him by what he contributes to it—and by both tests you're doing all right.

JOHN: I had thought so, too.

VOICE: This is all well and good if family and community were the highest claim upon you. They may think that you own what you earn and be satisfied with a good slice of it. But God is not mocked. He knows that He owns everything.

JOHN: That would make a difference.

VOICE: Actually, John, it might not make a difference in how much you claim as an income tax deduction—

JOHN: But it might make a difference in me.

TEMPTER: So I fear.

vi
SLOTH

As the Tempter and the Voice approach, John is discovered at a desk that is heaped high with books and manuscripts, and John, in an attitude of intense concentration, is rifling through a great sheaf of papers.

JOHN: Is there no end to this thing? I'll never get it finished.

TEMPTER: What time is it?

VOICE: It's late.

JOHN: Everyone else turned in hours ago, but here I am as usual: stuck with all this work.

TEMPTER: We'd better not bother John just now.

VOICE: Why not?

TEMPTER: He's busy.

VOICE: Yes, I know.

TEMPTER: Let's come back later.

VOICE: He'll still be busy. He's always busy.

TEMPTER: What's the point in interrupting him, then? We're not on the lookout tonight for a busy man. We want a lazy one. Our object was to talk about sloth, remember?

VOICE: I remember very well: we want to talk about sloth; and that's precisely why I want to talk with John.—*John!*

JOHN: Couldn't you come back another time?

VOICE: Name one.

JOHN: I could perhaps work in an appointment for you three weeks from now.

VOICE: In that case, we'll talk to you now. Now's as good a time as any other.

JOHN: Please excuse me if I seem a bit inhospitable. The point is that I've been slaving on this magazine article for a month, and it's no go. The material for it is here, but I just can't seem to pull it together.

TEMPTER: Yes, John, I've been watching your struggles with a good deal of sympathy. You almost finish one draft, then because it doesn't seem quite right, or because you get a new idea, you scrap it and start another.

JOHN: I work like a dog.

VOICE: John, you're a slothful man.

TEMPTER: Slothful? Have you lost your mind?

JOHN: I've been accused of many things, but nobody before ever accused me of being lazy.

VOICE: I didn't say you were lazy. I said you are slothful. And although laziness is one form of sloth, it's far from being the only form.

TEMPTER: Don't let him play with words, John. Insist

on following Webster, and Webster says that sloth means laziness. And if you want to see the living embodiment of it, don't look at John; look at John's kid brother.

JOHN: Yes, look at Junior! That good-for-nothing slug-a-bed, loafing his way through life. A pity his first wife left him all that money when she died. He hasn't lifted a finger since.

VOICE: I agree, John, your younger brother is a first-class loafer. He's guilty of sloth, all right. It's a fact I've been trying to impress upon him for quite some time.

JOHN: Not with any notable success, I'd say.

VOICE: Granted. But it's a fact I've been trying to impress upon you, too, John—with hardly any more success.

TEMPTER: How you can stand there and accuse my hard-working friend of sloth is more than I can fathom. Look at the hours he puts in.

VOICE: Isn't it just possible that the two of you are confusing "being busy" with industriousness?

TEMPTER: You and your subtle distinctions!

VOICE: Nothing subtle about it. I'm simply pointing to the fact that a lot of people, just by being perennially busy, manage to conceal from themselves the fact that fundamentally they are slothful. Now your younger brother is an obvious case of sloth in the form of laziness, disinclination to work. He gets up late, lounges around, attempts little, does even less.

JOHN: Like one of the French kings, that brother of mine could—if he ever got up the energy—write in his diary: Day before yesterday, *rien;* yesterday, at the races; today, *rien.*

VOICE: As I said, your younger brother is an obvious case.

TEMPTER: I know you aren't fond of him, John. But let's be fair. He used to work hard—mighty hard. He's entitled now to some leisure. Every man's entitled to leisure sometime in his life. But if you listen to some people (present company *not* excepted) you'd think the point in life is always to be up and at 'em. Nose to the grindstone all the time.

VOICE: That's not my idea at all. I'm a great believer in leisure. You might just recall how insistent I've always been on the idea that Sunday is a day of rest.

TEMPTER: Sunday spent twiddling the thumbs?

VOICE: Again, that's not my idea. Leisure can very well involve activity—it usually does. Sometimes leisure is just resting; other times it's quite strenuous activity.

JOHN: A hobby can be hard work.

VOICE: Quite so. But it's a carefully selected, different kind of work. As recreation, it has value in itself —physical, spiritual, cultural; and it has the further purpose of sending you back to your regular job restored and refreshed. So there's a distinction between leisure and laziness. And just as there's a distinction between leisure and laziness, so also there's a distinction between industriousness, on the one hand, and just being busy, on the other. John's younger brother is lazy. John himself is up to his neck in business. But they're both slothful —only in different ways.

TEMPTER: Anyone who works as hard as John has the right to resent being called slothful.

VOICE: I call you slothful, John, for—in spite of all your hustle and bustle—

JOHN: I know: you're going to say that, in spite of all my hustle and bustle, I don't really like to work.

VOICE: No, that's not what I was going to say. That's the sort of thing I might have said of your older brother, but not of you.

TEMPTER: Yes, let's talk about that old codger.

VOICE: I know, sir, that it accords very well with your methods of pointing the finger of blame elsewhere, but I insist on getting our attention back to the case in hand.

JOHN: But I *want* to talk about my older brother. He's a brother of whom I can be proud.

VOICE: Of your older brother I'll say only this: it's quite true that he works like a devil—with all due respects to our companion here. It's also quite true that he hates it like poison and can't wait for the day when he can retire; meanwhile, he forces himself to work, for he's haunted—or he thinks he is—by the fear of that coming rainy day.

JOHN: You're suggesting it's a sense of insecurity that whips him into the industriousness which he hopes will pay off?

TEMPTER: Well, his hard work is paying off beautifully in gilt-edged securities.

JOHN: And in the eyes of the community this makes him a fine example of thrift, industry, and sobriety.

VOICE: But because he hates it so—because essentially he's slothful—he's paying an awful price for those securities—a price in health, for instance (he's working himself to death), and a price in the matter of personal fulfillment. Always booked up, he never has time for a book—

JOHN: Or a show, a concert, or a ball game. He buys more and more land, but never has time to garden even a small plot of it.

VOICE: And think of the price his family has to pay.

JOHN: They rarely see him. And he's just announced that the family vacation will have to be put off to another year.

VOICE: Part of this, I'll admit, is just plain avarice. But much of it stems from sloth. He works like a Trojan, though he hates it, for he's too lazy to cultivate those hobbies and avocations and family relationships which could help to make him a real human being.

JOHN: I think I see the point. I have a younger brother who loafs because he's lazy and an older brother who *can't* loaf because he's lazy—too lazy to employ leisure time creatively.

TEMPTER: Aren't you forgetting that your older brother always maintains that he works now in order to have leisure later?

JOHN: I've often heard him say that he just can't wait to retire.

VOICE: John, your brother will never retire. Not voluntarily, at any rate. For the day he retires, he'll snap, go up in a puff of smoke. There'll be nothing left of him, for really there never has been very much to him. He hasn't worked to live; he has lived to work. He has, in fact, had no other life. Like all slothful people, he's bored with life, afraid of life. His own life is empty, so he works in the effort to fill up that big void.

TEMPTER: But none of this applies to you, John.

VOICE: Oh, yes, it does—though in a different form.

TEMPTER: But John likes work.

VOICE: Indeed, he does, and that's why his case is harder to diagnose.

TEMPTER: I suppose we're now going to be treated to some rummaging around in the depths of the unconscious.

VOICE: No, what I'm pointing to is near enough to the surface—though perhaps it takes a practiced eye to see it. You too have a big void in your life, John, and you too use work to try to conceal the fact that essentially you suffer from boredom.

TEMPTER: I don't know by what right you have introduced the subject of boredom into the conversation when we're supposed to be talking about sloth.

VOICE: I have good precedent for it. The word "sloth" in English happens to be a mighty inadequate translation of the Greek word *acedia*. Sloth in the sense of indolence, of disinclination to work, is part of what they meant by the term in the Middle Ages; but, as I have tried to show, it is linked in a subterranean way with *acedia* in the deep sense of that term. Historically, however, *acedia* is a concept that embraces far more than mere indolence.

JOHN: I recall that Chaucer speaks of "the rotenherted sinne of Accidie and Slouthe" and that *acedia*, though translated into English as sloth, originally meant something like dejection or boredom, the state of mind where everything seems "stale, flat, and unprofitable"—the world without rhyme and reason—so that nothing, or next to nothing, seems worth the effort.

VOICE: Right! And therefore I called you slothful, John, for, as I started to say long ago, in spite of all your hustle and bustle, and partly because of all your hustle and bustle, you've never really faced within yourself such questions as: Who am I? Why was I born? Where did I come from? Where will I go when I die? What, therefore, ought I to do in the meantime?—Already it's slothful of you to refuse to face these questions.

TEMPTER: You raise them with him often enough.

VOICE: But John always puts them from him. It's sloth never to wrestle with ultimate questions. John, you've never really asked yourself: What does it mean that you must die?

TEMPTER: Oh, I get the pitch! John, he wants to rivet your attention on death and on the future life. That's always the way with a regular joy killer. He'd like to get you thinking about the future life so that you don't really take full advantage of this life.

VOICE: Quite the contrary.

JOHN: How much should a man concern himself about the future—about death and the future life?

VOICE: He should concern himself with it only until he has conquered it. For not until he has conquered the future, can a man return to the present and be strong in it, take joy in it. Only then will a man have gained for himself a proper perspective, a proper sense of direction, a proper scale of values. For what good is it to work so hard and build so much if, as the Bible says, *Tonight shall thy soul be required of thee?*

TEMPTER: But the same Bible says, *Take no thought for the morrow*. That's a text for my side!

VOICE: It is not. It's precisely the man who hasn't settled the question about his ultimate tomorrow —which could happen any day—who is anxious about tomorrow.

JOHN: But I always keep so busy today that I never have time to think about any kind of tomorrow!

VOICE: There! You've said it with your own lips. You keep busy—to keep tomorrow at bay. That is, you work in order not to have to think. Thinking is too hard—and that's the form your sloth takes.

TEMPTER: You seem to be charging everybody with sloth.

VOICE: Not you, at any rate.

TEMPTER: Thank you! But it seems to me you've pretty thoroughly slandered a fine trio of brothers. The youngest you called a drone. The oldest you've called a drudge. And John here—

VOICE: For the last time I'll try to make the point clear. The younger brother hates work and won't work. The older brother hates work yet works all the time, for he knows nothing better to do. John here likes work—but he likes it only because it rescues him from having to think.

JOHN: Are you trying to say that I work as hard as I do so that I'll be too tired even to raise the question of what significance my work may have?

TEMPTER: But, John, your work is full of meaning. Think of all the significant themes on which you're writing. Think of all the causes you espouse.

VOICE: Perhaps there are too many causes, too many purposes. The presence of many purposes can perhaps obscure the fact that behind it all there is no fundamental purpose, no single aim which gives unity and direction to all the rest.

JOHN: But I do have a purpose! For the sake of that purpose I'm always on the move. I serve it with midnight oil. I serve it with the sweat of my brow.

VOICE: But do you know where that purpose tends? Not to know where it tends is not to have a total world view, not to have a satisfactory philosophy of life. That's why you, as a writer, have so many unfinished drafts. That's why you, as a person rich in possibility, have so little actuality. Let me put it this way. Your life is running riot in a thousand possibilities. There are really so many things that you can do that you end, essentially, by doing nothing. That is, you do lots of things, but you get little done, mostly because you've been too busy (that is, too slothful) ever to settle the question of what, fundamentally, you ought to do.

JOHN: You mean, the motor's racing, but it isn't in gear?

VOICE: That's exactly what I mean. You're involved in many things, yet on closer inspection your life lacks total engagement. Since there is no one fundamental thing that dominates you, you are dominated by a multiplicity.

JOHN: Like the knight in shining armor who jumped on his horse and rode madly off in all directions at once?

VOICE: Something like that. Your life is just a series of essays in the fragmentary. You do not grasp any one concrete thing—the little bit of actuality that could be done now, today, this very moment. Instead, you lose the moment, and you lose yourself in an abstract future. And that is why the sum of your life is a lot of projects—and a lot of unfinished drafts.

TEMPTER: I've several times impressed on John the need of a change.

VOICE: Yes, but John never permits himself a pause in which he might come to an understanding with himself. The urge he occasionally feels for a change gets no power over him, for the moment it comes, he's off on a new tangent, *trying to make that change*—even before taking thought about what kind of change might be needed. That's why his life is all projects—constantly shifting projects.

TEMPTER: To these projects he dedicates a lot of energy, a lot of talent.

VOICE: Yes, but since his life lacks essential dedication, all it comes to is activity—without accomplishment.

TEMPTER: Work is good for man.

VOICE: Yes, provided what you work for is worth working for. Without that, work is a curse and an awful waste of energy. John's great sloth is this: he's too busy to engage in the essential business of life, too busy to understand himself as the definite person he is, and too busy to be that person. He does not possess himself in an essential understanding of himself before God, but rather is possessed by a thousand possibilities. In sheer activity he has avoided the encounter with himself—and with God. A person John is not. His name is not John; it is legion.

TEMPTER: What do you recommend?

VOICE: In his case, leisure. John, I recommend that for a time you withdraw, that you deliberately and conscientiously do nothing—I mean, give yourself time to think: instead of racing the engine, let it idle.

TEMPTER: I hate to push myself, but there's a folk proverb to the effect that "the Devil finds work for idle hands."

VOICE: That's a risk worth taking, John.

vii
PRIDE

For a long time now John has been under heavy fire on the subject of his sins. We find him at home on a Sunday. His face is stern. There's a look of firm resolution in the set of his chin. Then—up pops the Devil!

TEMPTER: I can't deny, John, that a sort of change has come over you these last weeks. It worried me a bit at first. But it's all turning out very well, and I must say—I'm proud of you!

JOHN: Well, I have been doing a lot of thinking— spiritual stocktaking.

VOICE: And what is the outcome of all this self-examination?

JOHN: The outcome is that I'm a sobered man.

TEMPTER: You'll notice that the cockiness has gone out of John.

84

JOHN: I think I may say that I've learned some lessons in humility.

VOICE: Humility?

JOHN: Yes—as a result of our conversations.

TEMPTER: Remember, John, what an exalted opinion you used to have of yourself?

JOHN: Boy! I guess I was pretty intolerable.

TEMPTER: And intolerant!

JOHN: I'll say! I wonder now that my friends were able to put up with me.

TEMPTER: You always found some subtle way to let them know how good you were—

JOHN: And what a poor showing they made by comparison!

VOICE: Not all the ways were quite so subtle.

JOHN: Yes, there were a couple of instances, I'm afraid, when I was downright cruel. What a hypocrite I was!

TEMPTER: That picture you had of yourself as a paragon of virtue—

JOHN: Funny, how a man can be so deceived about himself.

TEMPTER: While in reality you were a pretty tarnished character.

VOICE: Demanding of others a standard you didn't yourself achieve.

JOHN: That's where hypocrisy comes in—and cruelty.

VOICE: Yet retaining through it all a high opinion of yourself, morally speaking.

JOHN: That was the self-deception and the dishonesty of it.

TEMPTER: Unconscious dishonesty, of course.

JOHN: For the most part, yes. I could congratulate

myself the way I did—because I'd never measured myself by ideal standards.

Voice: You measured yourself by human standards alone?

John: Yes, and by those standards it's easy for any halfway decent man to give himself a high rating for virtue.

Voice: Quite.

John: And I see now how self-deception about one's own morality makes it fearfully easy to be cruel about others' immorality.

Tempter: But all that's changed now!

John: Thank heaven, it is!

Tempter: Once you were so confounded proud.

John: But I'm more humble now—a reformed and chastened man.

Tempter: 'Tis a great and wonderful change.

Voice: Change? Well, some things are different—

Tempter: Yes, aren't you pleased?

Voice: In part. But what are the evidences of this great and wonderful reformation?

John: Well—

Tempter: You're embarrassing John. He doesn't want to boast.

Voice: Suppose you tell me then. You enjoy the role of advocate.

Tempter: There are three convincing indications, my worthy opponent, that you have achieved a victory in John.

Voice: Number one?

Tempter: John's whole outlook is different. You must rejoice to find that he's no longer the proud John. He's been humbled, I tell you. He's got a low opinion of himself.

VOICE: You think that ought to please me? How could it please me that John now has a low opinion of himself when, in fact, I myself have a very high opinion of John? It's the Devil's own mischief to confuse humility with self-depreciation. But first I want to hear all three points you allege as proof of John's reformation.

TEMPTER: Number two is that John has solemnly promised that things will be different from now on.

JOHN: Yes, I'm turning over a new leaf. I'm going to make a new man out of myself. It's just a matter of getting myself in hand and buckling down.

TEMPTER: Where there's a will there's a way!

JOHN: What a man ought to do a man can do. And I'll do it! You'll see.

VOICE: Yes, I suppose I shall. But now, what's evidence number three?

TEMPTER: Number three is that John is letting no grass grow under his feet. Only today John spoke very earnestly to several of his colleagues about the absolute importance of humility.

JOHN: The line I took made them a bit uncomfortable. They weren't accustomed to hearing me speak about—well, about spiritual things.

TEMPTER: But that was good for them!

JOHN: Yes, it was. They needed to hear that.

TEMPTER: I liked best, John, your moving plea to them that they too should reform. And I was thrilled by that picture you painted of how ideal a place the world would be if only people were less proud and more humble.

VOICE: John, did you manage to speak humbly of humility?

JOHN: Did I what?

VOICE: Not yet, John, can I discern any essential change in you. Outwardly you're different, but inwardly you're just about the same.

JOHN: But I—

VOICE: Once you thought you were good—and you were proud of your goodness. Now you've decided you're not good—and are proud of being humble.

JOHN: Proud of being humble?

VOICE: Yes, that's the final perversion: one's humility itself becomes the source of one's pride—and is the weapon one uses to chastise others.

JOHN: You mean that in the past I used the virtue of which I was so proud to beat others over the head, and that now I use my humility to beat people over the head?

VOICE: An exact statement of the case.

TEMPTER: Of all the defeatists I've ever met! You two are the prize pair. Can't you see, John, that this "perversion of humility" of which he speaks is only a passing phase in an altogether splendid spiritual development? Look, I know when I'm licked, so I'll make an elegant concession. The once proud John has humbled himself. For a starter at least, what more do you want?

VOICE: I want *John*.

TEMPTER: You want *John*? Well, there he is. Take him!

JOHN: I capitulated, didn't I?

TEMPTER: He's the picture of total surrender.

VOICE: John hasn't surrendered at all. Fundamentally John is just as much the prisoner of his own ego as ever he was.

JOHN: I'm completely confused. I thought I was doing

exactly what you wanted—and all I get is a bawling out.

TEMPTER: Go on, John. Let him have it!

JOHN: First, I'd heard that pride is a sin.

VOICE: It is.

JOHN: So when our talks had knocked the self-complacency out of me, I saw I wasn't the righteous man I'd supposed I was—

VOICE: So far so good.

JOHN: So I said to myself, "John, you've no right to be so proud."

TEMPTER: In the eyes of the community at large, you're looked up to as a model citizen, husband, and father. You don't drink, smoke, or swear. You vote, you pay your taxes, you work hard—

JOHN: Yes, but judged by any ideal standard, I don't come out so well. Once I understood the real meaning of lust and envy and covetousness, I had to admit to myself that I didn't measure up.

VOICE: Once again: so far so good. Our conversations were not wholly in vain.

JOHN: So then I resolved to mend my ways.

VOICE: Excellent! What then?

JOHN: Why, then I went to work.

VOICE: Successfully?

JOHN: Some days, yes. Some days I felt I was making a whale of a success out of my new character.

TEMPTER: I'll vouch for that. You'd hardly have recognized him. He was going great guns.

VOICE: And you felt God must be mighty well pleased with you?

TEMPTER: No, John was too modest to suppose anything like that.

VOICE: Too modest? Or maybe too busy with reforming himself (and others) to have much time for thinking of God?

TEMPTER: No, John's very religious.

VOICE: Perhaps especially on days when the reformer suffered a relapse?

JOHN: There were days, I'll have to admit, when I was a backslider.

TEMPTER: And I told John God was terribly displeased.

VOICE: Yes, I bet you did.

TEMPTER: I told him that because I know God wants people to be humble.

VOICE: And these little lectures of yours—they made John humble?

TEMPTER: Oh, you should have seen him grovel in remorse! It would have gladdened your heart.

VOICE: Nothing, in fact, could distress me more. Remorse is a fearful waste of energy.

JOHN: But I thought you wanted people to rue their past.

VOICE: Rue it, yes. But not to wallow in remorse over it—and go blubbering to your friends about it. I'm interested in something quite different from remorse. I'm interested in repentance.

TEMPTER: Remorse/repentance. What's the difference? Don't they come to the same thing?

JOHN: That you're sorry for your sins.

VOICE: No, they're different. In remorse, a man is only feeling sorry for himself. He hates his sin—but he hates it because it gives him a bad opinion of himself. In fact he hates this self of his which has shown itself capable of such things. The remorseful man doesn't shut his sins out. He shuts himself in with his sins.

JOHN: Oh, I know something about that! He ruminates. He broods. He despises himself for having been so weak.

VOICE: But all the time, you see, it's himself he's thinking about. He sits in judgment on himself. He takes himself to task. He Dutch-uncles himself. He solemnly promises himself to reform.

JOHN: And if he fails?

VOICE: He flogs his weary will and applies himself to the task with redoubled effort.

JOHN: And if that doesn't succeed?

VOICE: Then he despairs. Don't you see, John, the whole trouble with such a man is that he's stuck with himself? He can't get off dead center.

JOHN: But if that's remorse, what is repentance?

VOICE: Repentance honestly faces up to the past— but it does so in the presence of God. Faces it, confesses it, makes a clean break with it, forgets it. For the God who forgives sin *commands* him now to forget it—so as not to waste a moment more on it. Such a man, absolutely unburdened of the past, can now venture a fresh start, a free man.

TEMPTER: But if this "free man" should slip and fall again?

VOICE: Then he will get himself right humbly to his God again, and once again God will raise him up. But, John, I can't see—in this whole "reformation" of yours—that you've related yourself to God at all.

TEMPTER: That remark I don't understand at all. These days John is forever talking about God. "God demands this" and "God demands that" and

"How God must hate me for what I've been" and on and on and on.

JOHN: It's because of God that I'm making this big effort to remodel myself.

VOICE: Of all self-deceptions, John, this is the greatest. In your fight to combat a variety of sins you fall back into the root sin of them all: *pride*.

TEMPTER: But pride's the very thing he's been stripped of.

VOICE: On the contrary, his pride has never been cracked at all.

JOHN: Will the two of you stop talking over my head! I'm all mixed up.

VOICE: John, it's like this. Pride is not an act; it's not even a psychological attitude. It's a chronic disease of the soul; it's a status: the status of a man who shuts himself in upon himself and would be sufficient unto himself. However often the proud man may use the Name of God, essentially he only relates himself to himself; for he's the man who prefers to go-it-alone. Alone, without help from God, man wants to run life his own way, to be his own lord and master.

TEMPTER: Look, John, don't let that fellow forget that though you used to feel that way about yourself, you've been converted in the meantime.

JOHN: Yes, how about that? I've come to see that God—the real God—is Lawgiver and Boss, not me.

VOICE: That much was solid gain. But instead of breaking out of the enclosed circle of self, John, your old pride immediately reasserted itself in a new form.

JOHN: How so?

VOICE: Though you'd acknowledged God as Lawgiver, you said: *I* will live up to the Law. John, don't you see: that's still the old illusion of self-sufficiency. Your pride wasn't cracked, for you at once imagined that by self-discipline and ethical exertion you could fulfill the requirements from now on—and, more than that, even make up for lost time!

TEMPTER: But that's only right and proper. A man may have slipped, but surely he's entitled to reinstate himself.

JOHN: How?

TEMPTER: By extra labor.

VOICE: Extra labor leads only to a treadmill.

JOHN: Do you deny that morally I'm a hard worker?

VOICE: No, that I don't deny. But has your ethical exertion lifted you out of yourself? Isn't it a fact that your whole endeavor leads you either to presumption or to despair? When your striving seems to be succeeding, you're proud. When your striving suffers defeat, you're despondent.

TEMPTER: A perfectly healthy, perfectly natural rhythm.

VOICE: "Natural" it may be, but there's no health in it. The morally successful man grows presumptuous; the moral failure grows despondent. And John here, like so many men, swings between the two moods. He oscillates rather violently from the one pole to the other.

JOHN: Some days I'm on the crest of the wave. Other days I'm plunged into the slough of despondency.

TEMPTER: But, John, by intensifying your efforts you can always climb up out of those depths. You need the setbacks as a spur to renewed endeavor.

VOICE: What does he climb to?

JOHN: Why, I climb to new levels of moral attainment.

VOICE: Thanks to your own determination and effort?

TEMPTER: What else?

VOICE: And so, your very success in moral attainment only ministers to your pride, confirms you all the more in the illusion of self-sufficiency. The more you succeed, the less you feel any need for God.

JOHN: And what if I fail?

TEMPTER: You aren't going to fail.

VOICE: If you fail, you're back groveling in remorse —where you're just as riveted on *self* as when you imagined you were succeeding.

JOHN: Look, I'm not conceited.

VOICE: Nobody said you were conceited. I only maintain that you suffer from pride.

JOHN: But why do you call me proud?

VOICE: Because, in spite of everything, you still are —in the quite explicit sense of the word—*self-centered*. Mr. Tempter, I must hand it to you. In this case you've done very well for yourself.

TEMPTER: I flatter myself I have.

JOHN: See, he's proud too!

VOICE: Indeed, this was the cause of his Fall from Heaven.

viii

ORIGINAL SIN

John has been having a profitable session with his conscience, when—up pops the Devil!

TEMPTER: Well, John, I'm back again.

JOHN: But *he's* here too. And you know, they say "two's company, three's a crowd."

VOICE: When you're with me—

JOHN: I'm reassured and happy.

TEMPTER: And when you're with me—

JOHN: We do have interesting times! But when both of you are around, the misery of "three's a crowd" becomes very evident to me.

TEMPTER: What's troubling you particularly, John?

JOHN: Nothing in particular. Pretty much everything in general.

TEMPTER: Be more specific. I've yet to see a general problem which wasn't made up of a lot of particulars.

VOICE: Yes and no. We've talked about your sins in detail—

JOHN: I'll say you have!

VOICE: But actually these particular sins are only symptoms of something deeper.

TEMPTER: Ah, ha! I see he's preparing to cut the nerve of ethical endeavor. He's an awful pessimist, and by his dark allusions to "something deeper" he's only trying to discourage your commendable decision to reform. I, on the contrary, applaud the manly way you've set about meeting his requirements point by point or, as he would call it, "sin by sin."

JOHN: Just as you say, I've been trying to change things point by point, sin by sin; but, honestly, I haven't been getting very far. I still explode, inside of me if not outwardly, when my boss bears down on me. I still resent it when the woman next door sports something I can't afford to get for my wife. And, as one of you gentlemen—I can't place which one—said at an earlier session, "A pretty girl is still a pretty girl!"

TEMPTER: Oh, John, keep trying! You haven't been at this matter of reform very long.

VOICE: Actually, John is very perceptive. He's been at it long enough to see that there's a deeper difficulty. Man's problem is not just *sins* in the plural but *Sin* with a capital S. To be frank, the problem is Original Sin.

TEMPTER: What's that?

VOICE: Don't play so innocent. If it hadn't been for the likes of you, there never would have been such a thing.

JOHN: This is over my head. Let me in on what you're talking about.

TEMPTER: John, Original Sin is that tall tale about a couple named Adam and Eve who lived a long time ago and who did something God didn't want 'em to do, and God got so mad about it that He's had everybody behind the eight ball ever since.

JOHN: Oh, I'd always regarded that as just a fable.

TEMPTER: It is a fable, but the theologians—"inspired" by our friend here—have taken it so seriously that they've made it a cardinal point in religion.

VOICE: It's not a fable—

TEMPTER: What competent historian, geologist, or anthropologist would back it up?

JOHN: Yes, who would?

VOICE: I won't myself—in the terms you have in mind. But I back it up because it's a myth.

JOHN: That's what I said, a fable.

VOICE: That's not what I said.

JOHN: What's the difference?

TEMPTER: Watch him draw one of his fine lines again.

VOICE: It's not a fine line at all. A fable is a story which just plain isn't true. A myth is a story which, while it may or may not be true historically, has the purpose to say something that is everlastingly true—a truth so profound that it's pretty hard to grasp except in terms of a story.

JOHN: I've read the story of Adam and Eve. But what does it have to do with me?

VOICE: Why, John, you're Adam.

JOHN: Who? Me?

VOICE: In Hebrew Adam means "man."

TEMPTER: Enough of your playing with words.

VOICE: The story starts with God the Creator giving Adam the opportunity of sharing in His creative activity. Adam is to till the soil and dress the vineyard. And for intellectual activity he is to have the fun of naming the animals.

TEMPTER: How pre-scientific all this is!

VOICE: Is it? If a man can name something, generally he can control it. This is the relation between science and technics.

JOHN: Well, go on.

VOICE: Adam is at home with God. He walks and talks with Him. He's at home with nature. That's why the scene is set in a garden. He's at home with himself; that's why he feels no need of covering himself. Then someone very like this fellow intrudes himself into the picture.

TEMPTER: Yes, I know; masquerading as a snake he suggests to Eve that they eat an apple from a tree they weren't supposed to touch.

VOICE: The Bible doesn't specify that it was an apple, incidentally. But anyway, that's not the important thing that the intruder suggested.

JOHN: I must have missed something in the story.

VOICE: The temptation was: *Ye shall be as gods.*

JOHN: Ah, back to the old temptation to self-sufficiency, eh?

VOICE: Man decides that he can run his life, manage his world, be his own god.

TEMPTER: You're drawing a great deal out of the mere eating of an apple!

VOICE: But it was the fruit of the tree of the knowledge of good and—

TEMPTER: Yes, knowledge is virtue. The more men

know the better men are. For my money, this represents the beginning of human progress.

VOICE: You've deceived generation after generation with that line.

JOHN: Sounds all right to me. My school motto was *"Excelsior!* Onward and Upward."

VOICE: May I remind you that the fruit was the fruit of the tree of the knowledge of good *and* evil. Your idea—the more knowledge, the more goodness—is too naive. A college chaplain was once asked whether the young people today are better or worse than a generation ago. He answered: *Yes.*

JOHN: I don't get you.

VOICE: You see, the more people know, the better they can be—and the worse. And that applies to knowledge of morality, too. Even a professor of ethics is not necessarily a good man.

JOHN: I'm no professor of ethics, but this gives me a clue as to myself. Maybe that's why, in spite of our informative conversations on the Seven Deadly Sins, I still seem involved in all of them.

TEMPTER: I can see he's going to spin out the whole story. Why don't we get on with it?

VOICE: Well, now that Adam and Eve have issued their declaration of independence, they try to make a go of things on their own. Adam avoids conversation with God—even ducks into the bushes to evade the encounter.

JOHN: I guess he didn't want to talk about religion.

VOICE: I'm reminded of a young lady who told her pastor that a year ago she lost her religion, and he asked her: "What was the significant change in your conduct a year ago?"

TEMPTER: Let's get back to Adam. There was a significant change: he was freed from bowing and scrap-
ing before a fearsome God. John, you can have
that freedom, too. I hold with Swinburne: "Glory
be to man in the highest. Man is the master of
things."

VOICE: Wait a minute! Just remember how the story
worked out. Adam's attempt to separate himself
from God soon resulted in his separating himself
from his only neighbor.

JOHN: Oh, I can picture the family row when Adam
tried to pass the buck and blame the whole thing
on Eve!

TEMPTER: *Cherchez la femme!*

VOICE: But although Adam would deny responsibility
by shifting the whole thing to Eve, he still doesn't
feel comfortable within himself. And although
Eve tries to exonerate herself by pointing to the
serpent, she can't shake off her sense of implica-
tion either. Both of them want to cover up. Hence
the fig leaves.

TEMPTER: Almost Freudian! In any case, I maintain
that God shouldn't have put that tree there in
the first place.

VOICE: There you have it, John. Nobody will admit
guilt himself, but everybody stands quite ready
to volunteer the information as to who the guilty
party is. You see, man's deepest mystery is his
openness—upwards toward God, outwards toward
neighbors. Himself a person, he was made for
person-to-person communication. But once the
relationship with God is disturbed—the lines of
communication broken, this immediately reflects
itself in a disturbance of the relationship with

neighbors. Instead of mutual conversation we get people, thrown back upon themselves, issuing bitter communiqués, hurling at each other accusations, ultimatums, anathemas. But the disturbance in the God-relationship, reflecting itself in disturbed human relationships, reverberates further still: man's relationship with physical nature gets out of kilter too. All of life takes on a different aspect. The cool delights of Eden are replaced by bitter sweat and toil. From the unity with nature of the garden scene, man is barred by the flaming sword of cherubim. Men who would dominate nature and be gods, chop down the forests, destroy the watershed, cause the erosion which creates the dust bowls—

JOHN: I know—which makes poverty where there might have been plenty and produces the struggles between the "haves" and the "have nots." Man against man, brother against brother.

VOICE: If you will, Cain and Abel. Pride in the first generation breeds murder in the second, and by the tenth generation the whole world is ripe for the flood.

JOHN: For that matter, we've finally found a way, through probing nature's deepest secret, to split the atom and blow up the face of the earth.

VOICE: The history of man from Adam to atom.

TEMPTER: *Very* funny. And a very sorry picture our friend has painted. He's even coached theologians to say that man is totally depraved.

VOICE: I didn't supply them with those precise words —and would prefer myself not to use them because they're easily misunderstood. But in fairness to the theologians: by total depravity not even the "gloomiest" of the theologians meant that man is entirely depraved, but that every aspect of his nature, every faculty, has been somehow distorted, twisted. It's not that the total man is totally depraved but that sinfulness has somewhat crippled the total personality. No part of man's constitution has proved immune. Since man is a psychosomatic unity, when he falls, all of him falls, not just part of him.

JOHN: But I've always heard that it's the body that's evil, whereas the spirit or soul is essentially intact.

VOICE: John, that's exactly what these theologians were concerned to contradict. Whether you like their phrase or not, man's trouble is essentially a spiritual deflection. It's not that an evil body leads the noble spirit astray. It's almost the opposite: when the good spirit goes bad it involves its good body, as well as itself, in a revolt against God. Of this primary revolt—the revolt of spirit against God—the revolt of the bodily appetites against reason is a bitter and inevitable byproduct. Men who will not be governed by God soon find that they themselves can no longer govern their appetites—or else manage to do so, after a fashion, but only by taking totalitarian measures to repress the appetites altogether. Whichever way it goes, it makes a poor, stunted thing of man—a caricature, almost, of the splendid thing he was destined to become.

JOHN: This isn't easy to follow.

VOICE: Does it help at all if I put it this way? Satan's opening gambit, you remember, was: *Ye shall be as gods.*

JOHN: Stop right there! That doesn't tempt me. I've never imagined I was God, nor have I wanted to be God.

VOICE: No? Listen, John—and this will take some time. The distinctive thing about you and about every human being—that makes you a *man* and not a mouse or a stone—is your peculiar relationship to God, a relationship every man has to God though he be unconscious of it or even deny it. In even his wildest moments of conceit, man simply cannot get it through his head how great he actually is. You were made *by* God, *for* God. You were made, in other words, for unending fellowship with your Maker. This means: you're not just an animal, though you are also an animal. And there's nothing wrong about being an animal; it's just that you're more. Like the animals, you're animated, you've got flesh and blood, you're immersed in time and space, you die. Unlike the other animals, however, you're partly above time.

TEMPTER: Metaphysical subtleties!

VOICE: You've got a watch strapped to your wrist; you can tell time. Time can sometimes hang heavy on your hands; yet often you find that you have hours to kill; and at other times you bitterly complain that there is not time enough. And yet you know all the time, dimly at least, that at some point your "time" will come; and it is this that bothers you. This means that, although you are *in* time, you partially transcend time; and this makes for a qualitative difference between you and your nearest competitor, the chimpanzee!

TEMPTER: You needn't labor this point with John. I've made it clear to him that he's much, much more than an animal.

VOICE: How well I know! You've volunteered to make him a god! And, John, here is my whole point: the very fact that you're not just one of the creatures has itself made possible your succumbing to the temptation to forget your creatureliness and to comport yourself as if you yourself were sovereign lord of life. In short, you make yourself the center of meaning. This is Original Sin; from it, all other sins originate.

JOHN: When the two of you get talking, you sure do blow things up big. Hyperbole seems to be your element.

VOICE: You think we exaggerate? That's the strange thing about men. They either drastically underestimate themselves or else fantastically overestimate themselves. Sometimes they try to convince themselves that they're only animals—to justify themselves in behaving as such (though it slanders the beasts to describe what human beings do at their worst as "bestial"); and sometimes they pretend to an absoluteness and sovereignty, in judgment and decision, which altogether denies their finite character. In your present mood, John, you won't believe it; but what men do has cosmic consequences—for good or ill—and nothing happens on earth without its echo in eternity.

TEMPTER: [*Dryly*] Quite a speech!

JOHN: No, I want to hear him out. Speak as long as you like.

VOICE: Well, we're about ready to tie this discussion

up. Let's attempt a summary statement. Man is unique in all creation. Though *in* time and though bound to earth in multiple ways, man is partly *above* time, which means he is *en rapport* with the Eternal, with God. His true center, his true happiness, is in God on the eternal level. Only by being in proper relation to God can man become that which he is destined to be. If you'll grant this point for a moment, then it will be easy for you to see what sin is, in its root.

JOHN: Yes. Let me make a stab at trying to define it. The root of sin would then be man's attempt to find in himself, in this world of time and change, that center for his being and conduct which actually lies in God, in eternity alone.

VOICE: *Bravo!* It once took a commission of archbishops, bishops, and priest-theologians nearly a month to come up with so clear a definition! And this was all I meant—no more, no less—by saying that man desires to be his own god. This is the primal temptation—and the origin of sin. Man lets himself be beguiled into imagining that life can be fuller and brighter—more secure—if only he will declare his independence, emancipate himself from restraint, and take the reins of government into his own hands. Precisely a spiritual temptation. One sins through defiance.

JOHN: That may be. But I can testify that the flesh also makes its claims.

VOICE: Right you are. Only a disembodied spirit is capable of sheer defiance, a purely spiritual sin. Man, on the other hand, isn't spirit alone. He's a compound of both spirit and flesh. Therefore, his revolt is never purely spiritual, never simply a matter of proud defiance. Always an element of sheer human weakness—weakness of the flesh —is involved too. Nor did this element in sin escape the wisdom of the Hebrews. With sure understanding of the complexity of temptation and sin they wrote: *When the woman saw that the tree was good for food, and that it was pleasant to the eyes, and a tree to be desired to make one wise, she took of the fruit thereof, and did eat, and gave also unto her husband with her; and he did eat.* How superbly, therefore, the Book of Genesis recognizes that we sin partly through pride or defiance (it was a tree to be desired to make one wise), partly through the weakness of the flesh (it looked good, it tasted good). Man's sin is always an admixture of spirit or defiance and of weakness or flesh. Otherwise expressed, it's always an admixture of freedom and of fate, of culpable desire and of destiny.

TEMPTER: All right. I still say, it paints a pretty hopeless picture. Man is trapped. As a matter of fact, I think I can use this line of yours. If John is all this depraved, you can't legitimately hold him to account for anything. After all, he inherited all this. He was born that way. The cards were stacked against him from the start.

JOHN: [*Eagerly*] Sure, since I'm the product of bad heredity and bad environment, I don't see how I can be held responsible.

VOICE: If this were altogether true, how could he tempt you—or, for that matter, how could I pull you the other way?

JOHN: You mean I'd have no problem of conscience?

VOICE: Exactly. An essentially evil man could not be tempted by *evil,* and would, by the same token, be deaf to the call of anything higher. Perhaps I'd better explain to both of you something about this myth we've been exploring. If it were literal history, the tale would read: once upon a time men were good; then at a definite moment something went haywire; and now men are hopelessly bad. One, two, three! But when we regard it as myth, we are saying that all parts of the story are true at all times. John, you at this very moment, are Adam in the garden, and Adam just kicked out of the garden. If you want the traditional technical terms for it, you bear simultaneously the marks of original righteousness and of Original Sin.

JOHN: You mean I'm schizophrenic?

VOICE: Well, as a matter of fact you are a split personality.

JOHN: You mean half of me is bad and half of me is good?

VOICE: No, you aren't compartmentalized. Having come from the hand of God, you're all good; but in your flight from God, you're bad—in spirit as well as in flesh. You and your world have departed from the course for which it all was intended.

TEMPTER: Well, granting all this, this simply means that John has to ride out the storm. When he's pulled the good way, your side scores; when he's pulled the other way, I suppose I score. So, John, you might as well relax. Take it easy!

JOHN: You mean I'm not free in all this?

TEMPTER: You're really not.

JOHN: But I feel free.

TEMPTER: Yes, but it's an illusion—from which I'd gladly disenchant you; for it ladens you with a burden of guilt-feelings you ought really not to have to bear.

VOICE: John, he's half right. Half-truths, incidentally, are the Devil's stock in trade.

JOHN: What do you mean, he's "half right"?

VOICE: Well, sin gathers momentum as it goes; there is a carry-over from generation to generation; it gains tremendous cumulative power. And in every decision you're called upon to make, you're conditioned by the world in which you were born— a world which already was warped before you got here, a world which lost no time in warping your attitudes, a world which has a false set of values —a set of values it's very difficult for a man to buck. Hence, the strong tendency to adjust and conform.

TEMPTER: But that's what I say, there's nothing John can do about all this.

JOHN: Evidently not. I'm just a victim of circumstances.

VOICE: We might be tempted to say this were it not for the fact of "goodness." Look all around you. There are people who successfully buck the tide of social pressure—and men who after years of personal wrong-doing really change.

JOHN: I must say, when I'm confronted with the necessity of making a choice, I feel free.

TEMPTER: And when you make what he calls a bad choice—

JOHN: I feel guilty.

TEMPTER: A complex only. It won't stand up under analysis.

VOICE: Let's concede, John, that much guilt-consciousness is morbid, merely a complex. On the other hand, isn't it just possible some guilt feeling has its foundation, actually, in *guilt*? You're wiser than this fellow here who's trying to whitewash you entirely. If you accept his absolution, you do so by renunciation of your own freedom. Don't let him or anybody else trick you out of your most precious possession: freedom, with all that it entails—decision, risk, responsibility, and guilt.

JOHN: Well, if I'm free, as you say I am, why am I not free to do what I want to do: make a new man of myself?

VOICE: You're not that free, John; for while you yearn for a change, in large measure you've acquired what the psychologists call a "set." You're set in your ways, entrapped in your own previous bad choices and those of your parents, your society, and your world. And every new bad choice you make, John, though it always has an element of "freedom" in it, is partly predetermined by all that you have been and are. And every bad choice you make—a compound of weakness and of defiance, of destiny and of active decision—confirms you in a habit and contributes to the warpedness of the world which in turn makes it more difficult for you and others to make right choices in the future.

JOHN: Sounds like a vicious circle. Is there no way to break it?

VOICE: Yes. If there weren't, I'd never have brought

the subject up; but we'll have to meet again if I'm to explain it fully. Here I can only hint. Two great continuous performances are going on in the world. We have just aired one of them: the mutual interaction of sin, a drama of which our companion here is the director-producer. I'd like to talk a little about the other drama, a sort of love story—I'm a member of that troupe.

TEMPTER: You asked for it, John. Brace yourself for pulpit pathos!

VOICE: Adam may have tried to separate himself from God, but God never gives up on man. He's indefatigable.

TEMPTER: Don't I know!

VOICE: The very fact that in temptation you're troubled and that in sin you find no peace is proof of the second fact that, while you can depart from God, you can never be quit of Him. The Presence of God you may lose, but you'll never find His Absence. Which is to say, God is in pursuit.

TEMPTER: He's out to get you.

VOICE: Out to get you, John, but in a sense your bad conscience blocks out from view. He's out to get you but only to reclaim and reinstate you.

TEMPTER: *The wages of sin is death.* It won't be fun if God catches up with you, John.

VOICE: That's the voice of experience speaking, John, and he's right. Fun it won't be. The death of the gods is always a catastrophe. But, as Nietzsche said, "Where there are no graves, there can be no resurrections." The god called John has got to die before the child of God whose Christian

name is John can arise—the same man, yet radically transformed.

JOHN: *Re*-formed, you mean. I've got to reform myself before God and I can meet.

VOICE: There you're as wrong as sin. A man can't lift
himself out of the mire in which he's stuck by his
own bootstraps.

JOHN: But God could?

VOICE: And does. That's the drama of redemption.
God in His love—made known supremely in
Christ—shows Himself as a love "so amazing, so
divine" that He out-allures all the tawdry allure-
ments of the world; and thus the miracle occurs
that He elicits from man a responding love and
trust whereby a man is clean, lifted out of himself as center, and now finds a new center in the
all-holy, all-desirable God. That's no more than a
hint, but it's the essence of the drama of redemption. My best advice is: Come and see.

JOHN: What's the price of admission?

VOICE: Nothing.

TEMPTER: But there's a catch in it.

VOICE: Yes, there is—as I've already indicated. The
First Act isn't very pleasant, but without it the
rest of the play is unintelligible. We call the First
Act "Judgment"—diagnosis, if you will, and diagnosis must precede cure. A man has to see what
he's really like and know his need before—

JOHN: Oh, I see why you've been hammering away
at me these last few weeks.

TEMPTER: Ah, he enjoys that.

VOICE: As a matter of fact, I don't—though it's all in
my day's work. Not my proper work but a neces-

ORIGINAL SIN   111

sary prelude to it. And many of our clients finally let down their guard and accept our diagnosis—

TEMPTER: You've done that, John. Yet you yourself have said that you're not much better.

VOICE: That's only half of it. Diagnosis, though a necessary preliminary, is not yet treatment and cure. The hardest part of all for the self-centered man yet remains.

JOHN: Something else he has to do?

VOICE: Something he has to allow *to be done with him*. The Good Physician is willing to heal you, if you will lay bare your wounds and follow the course He prescribes. This means that *He* is the doctor, not you. And this comes close to the heart of the ailment: self-centeredness. God would recenter you around Him rather than around yourself and the world.

TEMPTER: He wants you to be other worldly, you see. Nice prospect!

JOHN: Sounds that way to me.

VOICE: Yes, other worldly in the sense that God would have you live on a level beyond that of this world, deriving both your standards and your strength from a transcendent realm and giving your allegiance to the heavenly country—

JOHN: But I like this world, and I'm for this country.

VOICE: God likes it too—as the Advent of His Son ought to have made clear. He wants you to enjoy it and work with Him to redeem it.

JOHN: Didn't Jesus say something about being *in* the world but not *of* it?

TEMPTER: That's fuzzy. You're either in it or out of it.

VOICE: No, you're to be very much in it—the way a pioneer is in a frontier land: he seeks to make it, as much as may be, like the homeland. You're to be, as St. Paul says, *a colonist of heaven.* Your *citizenship is in heaven*—that's where your final allegiance is; heaven's your destination—that's where you really belong; but meanwhile you find yourself, by God's appointment, in a foreign outpost as an ambassador for Christ, where, acting on instructions from home, you carry out His mission. Or, to change the figure a bit, on earth you're a soldier for Christ, a member of His foreign legion, fighting to recover for the King enemy occupied territory.

TEMPTER: A very lofty role for one who's supposed to be so sinful!

VOICE: It's *sinners* God uses as colonists—or He wouldn't have anybody to work with. But His men are not just sinners. They're sinners who've owned up to their sins and have been humble enough to let God forgive those sins, accepting their new status as a gift from God and not as a reward of merit. They're sinners who, in simple reliance on God, combat sin as best they can wherever they find it, in themselves and in others, and who do not perplex themselves overmuch about the results, their successes, or their failures, because they have both the boldness and the humility to believe that it is not they who bear God but God who bears them.

TEMPTER: John, that's degrading. It makes you dependent on someone else. You don't need to be dependent. You can be your own master.

JOHN: [*Musingly*] Your own master . . . *Ye shall be as gods.* [*Then with sudden insight*] Now I know who you are!

EPILOGUE

We don't know whether there is a Devil, but we know a good deal about his methods.

He never directly invites a man to do evil; most characteristically, he presents the evil as good. Wrath he presents as righteous indignation; lust as "being natural"; envy as standing up for one's rights; covetousness as industry compounded with altruism; sloth as either busyness or leisure—whichever suits his purpose; gluttony as proper concern for one's well-being; pride as a sense of moral progress.

He is too wise to propose a totally perverse aim; what he dangles before the inward eyes is a genuine good, the exercise or enjoyment of which is a valid part of life. He seeks, by exaggerating its importance and minimizing countervailing claims, to induce a preoccupation with the particular aim. Temptation is then primarily *a fixation upon a part at the expense of the whole*.

Such a fixation is not achieved all at once. The Tempter is patient. The planting of an idea, the picturization of a fulfillment (the human imagination is very fertile), a wistful passing thought—he may regard as a sufficient day's work with a given client. If such thoughts are oft repeated, they feed on themselves; the Tempter need hardly trouble to renew them. If they are not dealt with constructively or if they are suppressed, they sink into the unconscious depths, where they exercise an even more powerful influence on the personality. If sufficiently magnified, impulses thus bottled up in the unconscious mind induce virtually compulsive actions which rob the conscious mind of its leadership and make it subservient. And to excuse the destructive conduct that follows, rationalizations are then hastily constructed. The man so preoccupied can become oblivious to consequences or to the opinions of others, even going so far as to take it for granted that other people's standards are no higher than his, and that, in his headlong course, all is well.

Some religious traditions are so activistic that they are insufficiently concerned with inwardness in the cultivation of goodness; others are so concerned with the sinfulness of "impure thoughts" that suppression of the same is encouraged. In either case the Devil rejoices.

Similar results are observed in cases where the compulsiveness stems from sociological influences upon men's conscious and unconscious life. A given culture, or stratum of that culture, can provide a matrix which provides false aims and ideals for the individual. A social fixation, a popular preoccupation, can make it difficult, if not impossible, for the individual to "leap over the wall" into freedom of aspiration and action. Thus some thinkers who might deny belief in a personal Devil nevertheless recognize the category of the *demonic* in the warped structures of our common life.

So both from personal habits of thought and "vain imaginations" and from social distortions, Everyman can cry with St. Paul: *I see another law in my members, warring against the law of my mind. . . . What I would, that I do not; but what I hate, that do I. . . . O wretched man that I am! who shall deliver me from the body of this death?*

One thing is clear: a man cannot deliver himself. The root trouble is self-centeredness. In his very struggle to replace vices with virtues a man's preoccupation with himself increases. In his reflection upon past guilty acts the weed of desire for repetition often grows up alongside of the flower of repentance. His growing self-consciousness about his moral state will make his evil more erratic, his good less attractive. And, as we have seen, he will alternate between pride and despair.

The cure must, in the nature of things, be one that lifts a man off himself as center and recenters him around an allegiance that will not destroy the self, but will inspire its richest fulfillment. A strong devotion to some person or great cause can achieve this in a measure. But a man cannot—and dare not—make himself totally beholden to any person or cause. The range of a man's possibilities is too great; human relationships are too transitory. Persons are not constant; causes fail or become demonic in their pretensions to righteousness. And insofar as a man, for a period, finds his meaning in a person or cause, he has to that degree lost his freedom. He may safely give himself only to God. God is constant; He is all-embracing in His concern for all that a man's possibilities could embrace. And if a man makes God the center of his meaning, he is truly free from the domination of his personality by anything of earth. He can then "sit loose" to the world and to "the changes and chances of this mortal life," even to the self with its tides of emotion, its deflections of purpose. Being free of self-centeredness, his self-fulfillment is not denied but guaranteed.

But can such a thing be? If not, our analysis of sin is to no effect. More than that, if there be no genuine cure for sin, analyzing it is to bad effect. The less said about it, the better. Rather the light-hearted frivolity of the "happy pagan"—too naive, too ignorant, too innocent to reckon of what weight sin is—than a heavy-hearted rumination which leads to unhappiness, frustration, and a fresh onslaught of temptation. All you can do with a man suffering from a definitely incurable disease is to make him as comfortable as possible. Precisely because secular thought knows no cure, it has—cannily enough—bent every effort to make men comfortable in their sins. Precisely because Christianity does know the cure, it is uncomfortably persistent in reminding men of their sins. Biblical religion alone can call sin *sin,* without being morbid.

Will God save us from our sins? How a man answers that question determines whether or not self-examination is a wholesome thing. For some it will be a prison; for others, the Forecourt of the Temple.

205-956-C-10.5